MACMILLAN MASTER GUIDES

MASTER GUIDES

GENERAL EDITOR: JAMES GIBSON

JANE AUSTEN	*Emma* Norman Page
	Sense and Sensibility Judy Simons
	Persuasion Judy Simons
	Pride and Prejudice Raymond Wilson
	Mansfield Park Richard Wirdnam
SAMUEL BECKETT	*Waiting for Godot* Jennifer Birkett
WILLIAM BLAKE	*Songs of Innocence and Songs of Experience* Alan Tomlinson
ROBERT BOLT	*A Man for All Seasons* Leonard Smith
CHARLOTTE BRONTË	*Jane Eyre* Robert Miles
EMILY BRONTË	*Wuthering Heights* Hilda D. Spear
JOHN BUNYAN	*The Pilgrim's Progress* Beatrice Batson
GEOFFREY CHAUCER	*The Miller's Tale* Michael Alexander
	The Pardoner's Tale Geoffrey Lester
	The Wife of Bath's Tale Nicholas Marsh
	The Knight's Tale Anne Samson
	The Prologue to the Canterbury Tales Nigel Thomas and Richard Swan
JOSEPH CONRAD	*The Secret Agent* Andrew Mayne
CHARLES DICKENS	*Bleak House* Dennis Butts
	Great Expectations Dennis Butts
	Hard Times Norman Page
GEORGE ELIOT	*Middlemarch* Graham Handley
	Silas Marner Graham Handley
	The Mill on the Floss Helen Wheeler
T. S. ELIOT	*Murder in the Cathedral* Paul Lapworth
	Selected Poems Andrew Swarbrick
HENRY FIELDING	*Joseph Andrews* Trevor Johnson
E. M. FORSTER	*A Passage to India* Hilda D. Spear
	Howards End Ian Milligan
WILLIAM GOLDING	*The Spire* Rosemary Sumner
	Lord of the Flies Raymond Wilson
OLIVER GOLDSMITH	*She Stoops to Conquer* Paul Ranger
THOMAS HARDY	*The Mayor of Casterbridge* Ray Evans
	Tess of the d'Urbervilles James Gibson
	Far from the Madding Crowd Colin Temblett-Wood
BEN JONSON	*Volpone* Michael Stout
JOHN KEATS	*Selected Poems* John Garrett
RUDYARD KIPLING	*Kim* Leonée Ormond
PHILIP LARKIN	*The Less Deceived* and *The Whitsun Weddings* Andrew Swarbrick

MACMILLAN MASTER GUIDES

D.H. LAWRENCE	*Sons and Lovers* R. P. Draper
HARPER LEE	*To Kill a Mockingbird* Jean Armstrong
LAURIE LEE	*Cider with Rosie* Brian Tarbitt
GERARD MANLEY HOPKINS	*Selected Poems* R. J. C. Watt
CHRISTOPHER MARLOWE	*Doctor Faustus* David A. Male
THE METAPHYSICAL POETS	Joan van Emden
THOMAS MIDDLETON and WILLIAM ROWLEY	*The Changeling* Tony Bromham
ARTHUR MILLER	*The Crucible* Leonard Smith *Death of a Salesman* Peter Spalding
GEORGE ORWELL	*Animal Farm* Jean Armstrong
WILLIAM SHAKESPEARE	*Richard II* Charles Barber *Othello* Tony Bromham *Hamlet* Jean Brooks *King Lear* Francis Casey *Henry V* Peter Davison *The Winter's Tale* Diana Devlin *Julius Caesar* David Elloway *Macbeth* David Elloway *The Merchant of Venice* A. M. Kinghorn *Measure for Measure* Mark Lilly *Henry IV Part I* Helen Morris *Romeo and Juliet* Helen Morris *A Midsummer Night's Dream* Kenneth Pickering *The Tempest* Kenneth Pickering *Coriolanus* Gordon Williams *Antony and Cleopatra* Martin Wine *Twelfth Night* R. P. Draper
GEORGE BERNARD SHAW	*St Joan* Leonée Ormond
RICHARD SHERIDAN	*The School for Scandal* Paul Ranger *The Rivals* Jeremy Rowe
ALFRED TENNYSON	*In Memoriam* Richard Gill
EDWARD THOMAS	*Selected Poems* Gerald Roberts
ANTHONY TROLLOPE	*Barchester Towers* K. M. Newton
JOHN WEBSTER	*The White Devil* and *The Duchess of Malfi* David A. Male
VIRGINIA WOOLF	*To the Lighthouse* John Mepham *Mrs Dalloway* Julian Pattison
WILLIAM WORDSWORTH	*The Prelude Books I and II* Helen Wheeler

MACMILLAN MASTER GUIDES

DEATH OF A SALESMAN

BY ARTHUR MILLER

PETER SPALDING

MACMILLAN

First published 1987 by
MACMILLAN PRESS LTD
Houndmills, Basingstoke, Hampshire RG21 6XS
and London
Companies and representatives
throughout the world

ISBN 0–333–41677–5

A catalogue record for this book is available
from the British Library.

13 12 11 10 9 8 7 6 5 4
05 04 03 02 01 00 99 98 97 96

Printed in Malaysia

CONTENTS

GENERAL EDITOR'S PREFACE

The aim of the Macmillan Master Guides is to help you to appreciate the book you are studying by providing information about it and by suggesting ways of reading and thinking about it which will lead to a fuller understanding. The section on the writer's life and background has been designed to illustrate those aspects of the writer's life which have influenced the work, and to place it in its personal and literary context. The summaries and critical commentary are of special importance in that each brief summary of the action is followed by an examination of the significant critical points. The space which might have been given to repetitive explanatory notes has been devoted to a detailed analysis of the kind of passage which might confront you in an examination. Literary criticism is concerned with both the broader aspects of the work being studied and with its detail. The ideas which meet us in reading a great work of literature, and their relevance to us today, are an essential part of our study, and our Guides look at the thought of their subject in some detail. But just as essential is the craft with which the writer has constructed his work of art, and this may be considered under several technical headings – characterisation, language, style and stagecraft, for example.

The authors of these Guides are all teachers and writers of wide experience, and they have chosen to write about books they admire and know well in the belief that they can communicate their admiration to you. But you yourself must read and know intimately the book you are studying. No one can do that for you. You should see this book as a lamp-post. Use it to shed light, not to lean against. If you know your text and know what it is saying about life, and how it says it, then you will enjoy it, and there is no better way of passing an examination in literature.

JAMES GIBSON

ACKNOWLEDGEMENTS

Cover illustration: *Max Wall and his image* by Maggi Hambling. Photograph © Tate Gallery Publications Department.

The author and publishers wish to thank the following who has kindly given permission for the use of copyright material: Elaine Greene Ltd on behalf of Arthur Miller for extracts from *Death of a Salesman* by Arthur Miller, Penguin Books Ltd Copyright © Arthur Miller 1949.

1 ARTHUR MILLER:
LIFE AND BACKGROUND

Arthur Miller was born on 17 October 1915, on East 112 Street, Harlem, Manhattan, New York City, into a prosperous Jewish family. His father, Isidore, who had been brought to America from Austria while still a small boy, never seems to have shown much interest in any of the arts, devoting most of his energies to his clothing business. The family was not strictly Orthodox in religion but the three children, Kermit, Arthur and Joan were brought up to respect the ethics and customs of their ancestors. Although he makes many references to such matters in his writings, Miller cannot be categorised as a Jewish writer in any limiting sense of the word. Indeed, in his childhood he gave very little indication that he would ever become a professional writer at all. His mother, Augusta Miller, who had been a schoolteacher and was very ambitious for all her children, was very disappointed in his lack of progress at school. Even at high school he remained a poor student showing little interest in anything except football and athletics.

In 1928, Isidore Miller became aware that trade was beginning to slow down with the approach of the Depression and decided, for economic reasons, to move from Manhattan to Brooklyn, which in those days was still rural, with a forest of elm trees in the Midwood section, near where the Millers lived. It is very likely that the young Arthur Miller enjoyed the move from built-up Manhattan to the open spaces of Brooklyn. It is also probable that the mature writer is expressing through Willy Loman his own regret at the destruction of the countryside which was taking place in the 1930s, the period in which, like Biff Loman, he was at high school.

There were not good times in which to begin a career. The Wall Street stock market collapsed in 1929 and destroyed business confidence. Credit became almost impossible to obtain. Banks went into liquidation, taking assets and savings with them. Over the next few years many business firms, including Isidore Miller's, were forced to close.

Arthur Miller graduated from high school with few qualifications and no skills except those of the football stadium and the running field. After a brief experience working as a salesman with his father he became a warehouseman, a waiter, truck driver and even, for a short period, a crooner at the local radio station. Although none of these jobs offered any career prospects they served to advance his education by acquainting him with many different kinds of people. It was at this stage in his life that he first became interested in politics. The Depression was affecting the lives of most Americans and its causes were hotly debated everywhere. Some people blamed the capitalist system, others accused the communists, while others denounced certain racial groups, especially the Jews. Thus it came about that the young Arthur Miller had his first taste of anti-Semitism but this did not deter him from joining in the discussion.

He was beginning to read widely, at first without much discrimination, often making chance discoveries of books that were to influence him. For instance, he picked up a copy of Dostoyevski's *The Brothers Karamazov*, thinking that it was a detective story. He read it on the subway as he travelled to and from work, thus finding his way into nineteenth-century Russian literature. After this, he began to choose his reading with greater care.

At seventeen he was beginning to write short stories, not in order to escape into fantasy but as a means of coming to terms with his experience. He gradually became aware of his need for academic discipline so, in spite of his unimpressive high school record and chronic shortage of money, he applied for university places. After several attempts he was accepted, in 1934, by the University of Michigan to study English, switching later to journalism, perhaps because that subject seemed to offer more obvious career opportunities. The fees were low but it was still necessary for him to work outside lecture hours to support himself. He washed dishes in the student cafeteria and worked at night in the office of the local newspaper.

While looking for a means of enlarging his income, Miller discovered his vocation as a playwright. The Avery Hopwood Foundation was offering a prize of $250 for the best original three-act play of the year written by a junior student. Undeterred by his limited experience of theatre he decided to enter because he needed the money. He had read some of Shakespeare's tragedies but nothing else and had seen only one play in his life. Nevertheless, he set to and finished his first play within a week. Then, not feeling sure that he had written it in the right style, he consulted a friend to find out how long such a work should last and what proportion of time should be allocated to each of the acts. To his surprise and pleasure he discovered that his play would fit inside the two hours normally considered correct and that the acts were properly balanced. He submitted *Honours at Dawn* in June 1936 and won the award. The following year, he repeated his success by taking another $250 for a play called *No Villain*. Both these remain in the library at the University of Michigan unpublished and unproduced since that time, but they contain themes and situations which foreshadow much of the later work.

Miller graduated as Bachelor of Arts in 1938. Before leaving Michigan he entered a play for the Senior Avery Hopwood Award of $1,000. The play, a reworking of *No Villain*, was called *They Too Arise* but failed to win the prize, perhaps because of its political viewpoint. It describes the difficulties of living in New York during the Depression. However, when it was submitted to the Theater Guild Bureau of New Plays it immediately won an award of $1,000. The Theater Guild, founded in 1919 to produce non-commercial plays of merit, was to have a great effect upon his career. From the work of the Guild there evolved the Group Theater, the membership of which included most of the writers, actors and directors who were to be associated with Miller in his early professional life.

Having discovered a talent and received recognition for it, Miller seemed to be set for a career in the professional theatre. In 1938 he accepted a job as writer in the United States Federal Theatre. This had been set up in 1935 by President Roosevelt as part of his New Deal to ameliorate the effects of the Depression. Its object was to employ writers, actors and designers in socially useful work – to bring the arts to the people. During its short existence the Federal Theatre was very successful and Miller found the experimental atmosphere and the democratic ideals to be congenial. Unfortunately, after considerable criticism from some politicians the project was closed down and he was unemployed once more.

By now, he was a family man, having married Mary Slattery, a fellow student at Michigan, in 1940. He tried to earn money by writing radio scripts, but found the work frustrating because of programme pressures which prevented him from injecting any ideas which were at all complex or controversial. Some of the longer scripts have been published but he made very little out of them. On the other hand, he was practising techniques which were to be useful in his later work, especially in a play such as *Death of a Salesman*.

During the war, Miller was exempt from military service because of a disabling football injury. After a spell working as a fitter in the Brooklyn navy yard, he was later directed into work as a writer on the script of a film about the training of American servicemen to be called *The Story of G. I. Joe*. This was never completed as planned, but in 1944 he published a book which incorporated much of the material he compiled from interviews with servicemen under the title of *Situation Normal*. In the same year, Miller's first play to be produced professionally was presented on Broadway. It was called *The Man Who Had All the Luck* and ran for less than a week. According to all the critics, it deserved its fate because of its conventional characterisation and clumsy construction – the usual faults of the novice playwright.

After this failure, he turned to writing in a different *genre* and in 1947 published his only novel, *Focus*, a tensely written story on the theme of anti-semitism. The skill with which it is written suggests that Miller could have remained a novelist, but in the same year his play *All My Sons* was produced on Broadway. This was not only a commercial success but received the New York Drama Critics' Award. A production of the play in London, in 1948, introduced Miller's work to a wider audience, and he now became widely recognised as a writer and was earning enough to live comfortably. *Death of a Salesman* was produced in New York in 1949 and also won the New York Drama Critics' Award. Later, it received the coveted Pulitzer prize for literary works of outstanding merit. Miller's international reputation as a master playwright in the eyes of critics and general public alike rests primarily on this play. After its initial success it has been regularly revived on the stage and in film and television versions in English and many other languages. It is regarded by many people living outside the United States as providing an insight into 'the American character' and the leading role is generally accepted as one of the major challenges for an actor. Of all his other work, only *The Crucible* approaches it in general popularity or critical esteem.

This play, based upon the witchcraft trials which took place in seventeenth-century New England, was produced in New York in 1953. Many people saw parallels between those trials and the proceedings of the Senate Un-American Activities Committee, which at this time was investigating the actions and opinions of those American citizens who were thought to be conspiring to overthrow the legally elected government of the United States. Among these people were some writers and actors known to Miller who were associated with the American Communist Party.

In 1954, while *The Crucible* was being produced in England and also in translation in several European countries, Miller was called to appear as a witness before the Senate Un-American Activities Committee. Pending their discussions, he was refused a passport to attend the opening of his play in Brussels. After some delay he was called to appear before the Committee but consistently refused to inform on people that he knew. In the course of the hearings he clarified his own viewpoint of the status of a creative writer within society, claiming that there must be freedom to choose any topic and to treat it in any style thought fit. This position was neither comprehensible nor acceptable to the Committee. In 1957, he was finally convicted of contempt of Congress for refusing to name suspected communists. Miller was given a suspended jail sentence and fined, but after an appeal to the Supreme Court the conviction was reversed. In 1958, partly in recognition of his stand for artistic freedom, he was elected a member of the American National Arts Institute of Arts and Letters and later awarded its Gold Medal for Drama.

In the meantime, Miller has paid a tribute to the great nineteenth-century Norwegian playwright, Henrik Ibsen, by producing a new translation of *An Enemy of the People*, a play which has some thematic similarities to *The Crucible*. Miller had always been an admirer and disciple of Ibsen, but feeling that the master's works were being neglected because their style had become old-fashioned, he modernised the play by condensing the five acts into three and simplifying the dialogue.

In 1955, two plays were produced in a double bill in New York. One of these was *A View from the Bridge* which was extended and presented in London at the Royal Court Theatre in 1956. It immediately ran into trouble with the British censor because of references to male homosexuality. Also in 1956, Miller's first marriage ended in divorce and he married the film actress, Marilyn Monroe, for whom he wrote the script of the film *The Misfits* in which she appeared with Clark Gable in 1960. Monroe's part was 'tailor-made' for her and based upon the characters in two short stories Miller wrote for *Esquire* magazine. This second marriage ended in 1961 and in 1962 Miller married his present wife Inge Morath, an Austrian-born photographer. The couple have remained together in a relationship that is professional as well as marital.

Two new plays, *After the Fall* and *Incident at Vichy* were both produced in New York in 1964. The first has autobiographical overtones and the characters are recognisable as being based upon real people, notably Monroe and Miller himself. The other play explores aspects of the Nazi persecution of the Jews in the 1940s but it also raises the question of personal responsibility for other people. In 1968, Miller's most obviously Jewish play, *The Price*, was produced in New York and subsequently in London. As so often in his work, the central relationship depicted is that existing between a father and his sons.

From 1969 to the present day Arthur Miller has continued to write and to travel but neither the plays nor the travelling, although interesting in themselves, are directly relevant to this book until 1983, when he went to China to direct the Peoples' Art Theatre in a production of *Death of a Salesman*. He subsequently published a book about this experience, *Salesman in Beijing* (Methuen, 1983). This production was perhaps a crucial test as to whether the play was limited in its appeal to audiences who knew and understood the circumstances of the United States in the post-war period, or whether it had a universal appeal irrespective of the national culture of its audience. On balance, the Peking experience seems to suggest that the play is a universal masterpiece.

In 1986 the play, *The American Clock*, was produced in London at the National Theatre. Written in 1980, and set in 1935, it is a re-examination of the American Depression which Miller believes has become romanticised by some people. The period between the Wall Street crash and the beginning of the Second World War provided him with a bitter and seminal experience from which he continues to learn.

Before leaving Miller's biography in order to concentrate upon the play it is necessary to consider how far it is ever possible to separate a writer from his work.

From about 1950 until the mid 1960s Miller was highly successful as a writer, but because of his political ideas he was open to attack from his opponents and misunderstanding by his friends. How far the opinions that he held at the time of writing may have affected the shaping of *Death of a Salesman* will be discussed later, but it is important to realise that Miller never wrote any of his plays as a parable to illustrate a political theory. This is not his way of working.

Most writers use their own lives as the starting point for their imaginative writing and Miller is obviously no exception to this. However, there are very important differences between biography and fiction and we must beware of confusing them, especially when there appear to be many similarities between the life and the fiction. At first sight, *Death of a Salesman* appears to be full of autobiographical references. Willy Loman, like Isidore Miller, is a business man with two sons who moves out to Brooklyn. Arthur Miller, himself, like Biff Loman, was a high school athlete but, for a long time at least, not much of a scholar. Isidore Miller worked for a time as a salesman on commission. Other similarities could be found if we took the trouble to look for them but the differences are greater in number and far more important. For instance, it is unlikely that Linda Loman is based upon Augusta Miller and in none of the plays does there seem to be a character obviously based upon Arthur's sister Joan. While Miller frequently used a pattern of family relationships involving a father with two sons, he treats the relationships in many different ways.

Above all, it is significant that the Loman family is not Jewish, although they could be played that way. It is interesting to note that the distinguished American–Irish actor, Thomas Mitchell (1892–1962), led a company on tour in America in which all the members of the Loman family were Irish actors who played the characters in their own accent.

2 FEATURES OF THE PLAY

2.1 REASONS FOR ITS CONTINUED POPULARITY

Death of a Salesman was Miller's third play to be produced on Broadway and was the second to achieve an outstanding success. It has been said that never a week passes without there being a production of *Death of a Salesman* taking place somewhere in the world. Not only has it won the Pulitzer prize but also other awards from institutions in America and elsewhere. The play is still being written about and discussed long after its first appearance. It is very unusual for a contemporary play to be esteemed immediately by serious scholars at the same time as it becomes popular with large audiences who merely go to the theatre to enjoy themselves. There are several reasons for this.

First, the play is undoubtedly well written in that it seizes the attention of the playgoer right at the start and keeps his interest until the end. Secondly, it is written in a generally *realistic* style, using situations and language likely to occur in real life. Although it is clearly set in the United States of the 1940s, it is acceptable to audiences everywhere because the characters and relationships within the Loman family are universally recognisable. Thirdly, the character drawing of the principal parts is such that good actors will respond to the challenge of playing them. The part of Willy, in particular, has been treated to different interpretations from Lee J. Cobb's 'walrus' to Dustin Hoffman's 'shrimp' (see Section 6), yet all these variations have been shown to be quite valid as might be expected of a truly classic part. Finally the *manner* in which the story is told excites the interest of the audience by letting them into the private thoughts of the central character, thus deepening their involvement with him and adding a dimension of *poetic theatre* to what is otherwise a realistic play.

2.2 ORIGINS

Miller is on record as having said that the first title for this play was 'Inside His Head'. This was because of an image that occurred to him of a face large enough to fill an entire proscenium arch. He began to wonder what would happen if this head could open up so that the audience could see inside – into the mind of a man. This image remained with Miller until the rest of the play was complete. Obviously, there were other components which had to be assembled before Miller could begin to write the play as we know it today. Some aspects of the family relationships (a father with two sons, for instance) had been used before in *All My Sons*, Miller's previous play, but were to be developed differently in the new work. In addition, there were memories of his own personal life in Brooklyn, of his work in New York during the Depression, and his acquaintance with salesmen of different kinds. All these combined with the original image to make up the play.

There is one other important and indeed unique feature of the play which owes its origin to Miller's past experience. He spent some years as a writer of radio plays. The radio playwright is able to make direct contact with his listeners and can appeal to their imagination, changing the time and location of the action as frequently as he may need to without the necessity facing a theatre playwright of requiring changes of setting, costumes and lighting. Furthermore, he can invite his listener to travel backwards and forwards in time, over vast distances of space and even to be, as it were, in two places at once or to see the same place simultaneously from more than one point of view.

In other words, the radio playwright can ask his listener to use his memory and imagination for the purposes of entertainment in exactly the same way as human memory and imagination tend to work when left to themselves. It seems clear that Miller's work in radio provided him with the basis for the timeswitch technique that he uses within this play.

2.3 THE TIMESWITCH

Although it is frequently said that the story of *Death of a Salesman* is told in a series of 'flashbacks', this is not strictly true. The flashback is a cinematic device which lacks the psychological subtlety and flexibility needed here. The term 'timeswitch', although not altogether perfect, indicates the effect Miller was trying to achieve.

Timeswitches occur inside Willy's mind, but are observed by the audience. Sometimes there is a change of location as well as of time, as when Willy 'slips back' to his last meeting with the Woman in Boston, while he is talking to Linda in Brooklyn. (This is in fact a 'double timeswitch', occurring inside a timeswitch back from the 1948 present to the 1931 remembered past.) This may *seem* complicated but it never bothers audiences in the theatre! These changes occur *only* for Willy himself. Although the other characters appear within these timeswitch sequences, looking and acting as they did in the past, their present-day (1948) selves are, of course, totally unaware that Willy is remembering them. It is a technique which has been immediately acceptable to audiences all over the world because Miller has simply dramatised what is after all a common experience.

We have all had memories that have been so remarkably vivid that we have almost felt that we were actually *living* an experience rather than remembering it. These are often triggered off by some unexpected similarity or coincidence. A total stranger suddenly encountered in a certain light may remind us of a person that we knew very well in the past, or we may hear music and find ourselves momentarily transported back in time to the place where we last heard it. Sometimes these memories are so intense as to make us believe that we have indeed 'slipped' in time or place or both. This is most likely to happen to people like Willy Loman who are elderly and under stress. Unlike Willy Loman, most of us never lose contact with the present time and place. Therefore, it can be said that every member of the audience has had some experience of the timeswitch, however rarely, and is ready to accept it as a device for telling a story in the theatre. The timeswitch differs from the flashback in one important way. Not only is it more psychologically convincing but in this play it is more than a storyteller's device. The tendency to live in a confused mental state, half-dream, half-memory, is an essential part of the character of Willy Loman, especially at this time in his life. Reality has become too hard for him to face, so he retreats into a happier past.

When Willy has drifted into one of his timeswitches, he retains its mood when he comes out of it. If the remembered events were happy in tone, then he comes out of the dream in a pleasant frame of mind, but if he was, for instance, angry with somebody in the past, then he will still be angry when he returns to the present. It is this that makes his behaviour inexplicable to those around him. For example, in Act Two he arrives at Charley's office to borrow money from him but, because of his timeswitch, is in a mood in which he is quite ready to have a fist-fight.

Before the detailed synopsis which will show us how the timeswitches operate to keep the scenes constantly changing so that the action may continue without a break, we must answer the question as to why Miller took the trouble to invent such a device. Why could he not have told the story in a more conventional way?

The best possible answer lies in the fact that Miller wished to tell the story through Willy himself, so that his character and state of mind are *always* clear to the audience. Secondly, the timeswitch technique makes it possible to change time and place very quickly without any need to lower the curtain or to change scenery and furniture to any great extent. Thirdly, Miller has always been an experimental playwright. He is also, as we have noted, a great admirer of the Norwegian writer, Henrik Ibsen (1828–1906). It is possible that *Death of a Salesman* is an attempt to apply modern stage techniques to the *social realist* drama which Ibsen developed.

Ibsen himself was an experimenter who took over the society melodrama of his time and put it to more serious use. In society melodrama, plays of the type being written in the nineteenth century by Henry Arthur Jones, Oscar Wilde and others, the dramatic interest of the story depended upon the revelation of a family secret. This secret is at first hinted at, then partially revealed and finally the truth is made known in such a way as to be destructive to one or more of the principal characters. By using the timeswitch Miller streamlined the nineteenth-century narrative technique and made it possible to dispense with lengthy explanations. In *Death of a Salesman* the audience need no explanations because they become aware of both past and present as the story unfolds.

2.4 CHRONOLOGY

Although the play tells the story of the last twenty-four hours in the life of Willy Loman, the action ranges over a very much longer period. If we accept that Willy Loman died sometime in the year 1948 then it is possible to use the many clues within the play to compile an approximate time-chart similar to that set out below.

1870–90   During the 'Wild West' period in the history of the United States Willy's father is making and selling his flutes as he travels from east to west.

1871   Ben Loman born.

1885   Willy Loman born.

1903   Alaskan gold strike. Willy could have gone to Alaska but meets Dave Singleman.

1912   Willy joins the Wagner company.

1914   Biff Loman born. Bernard born.

1916   Happy born.

1923   The Loman family move to Brooklyn, taking out a 25-year mortgage.

1928   Willy's best year for business as he remembers it. This was the year in which he drove the red Chevrolet.

1931   Biff fails to graduate, leaves high school and goes out to the West.

It is a tribute to the thoroughness of the playwright that it is possible to compile this chronology with reference to real events. For instance, Al Smith (mentioned in Act II, Sequence 2) was in fact nominated presidential candidate in 1928 after serving as Governor of New York.

3 SUMMARIES AND CRITICAL COMMENTARY

If we ignore for the moment all those scenes in the play which takes place 'inside Willy's mind', we are left with the 'public story', that is to say the story as it appears to the people around Willy who do not know what is going on in his mind. There are times when his actions appear to them to be strange or distressing or even frightening. It is an interesting fact that there is no character in the play who ever knows all the truth about Willy. Only the audience are in a position to understand and to judge Willy Loman at the end of his life.

3.1 THE PLOT

The plot is very simple. If we concentrate on the public story only, then it is easy to follow Willy Loman through the last twenty-four hours of his life. This 63-year-old salesman returns unexpectedly to Brooklyn one night having failed to reach his territory in New England. He is confused and frightened because he seems to have lost the ability to concentrate on driving his car. He disturbs his wife Linda, who loves him and has been worried about him for some time. She persuades him against his will to give up travelling and to ask his boss for a job in the New York office. The Lomans have two sons, both in their thirties, visiting the family home at this time. The younger, Harold but always known as Happy, lives nearby in his own bachelor apartment. He has a minor managerial job, but likes to give the impression of being rather important. The elder brother, Biff (the audience never get to know his real baptismal name), once showed great promise as an athletics hero at high school with a good chance of a place at a university, but has become a drifter getting a meagre living from casual work on the farms and ranches of the West.

The sons are disturbed by their father's strange behaviour. Happy says that Willy seems to spend a lot of his time talking to himself and he tells Biff 'most of the time, he's talking to you'.

At a time when Willy is not present, Linda reveals that he has lost his ability as a salesman, partly because of lost contacts and partly because he has become exhausted. His employers have stopped paying his salary and have made him work on commission only, just as if he were a beginner. He has not confessed this to Linda but she has found out that he has been borrowing money from their neighbour, a business man called Charley, in order to pretend to her that he is still on salary. She fears that he might commit suicide since she has reason to believe that he has already attempted it. The sons are distressed at her news but she rounds on them and points out that neither of them has shown much interest in their father since they grew up. She is particularly upset because Biff and his father have never got along together after a big row between them many years ago. Biff has constantly refused to tell Linda what the row was about.

In order to please his mother by settling down near at hand and also to make some attempt to come to terms with Willy, Biff agrees with Happy to try to set up a business venture with backing from Bill Oliver, an old employer of his. It is decided that they will approach Oliver at his office in New York on the following day and the first act ends on a note of optimism.

The 'public story' of the second act is a series of disappointments for Willy leading to his final defeat and death, although, as we shall see later when we come to consider the 'private story' in greater detail, Willy thinks that he ends his life in triumph.

Willy fails to persuade his boss to give him a job in New York and Biff not only fails to make the necessary contact with Bill Oliver but also commits a stupid and pointless theft which prevents him from ever trying again. They all meet up at the end of the day in a restaurant in the city. Willy and Biff once more misunderstand each other and a violent argument develops. Willy's behaviour becomes inexplicable and embarrassing to Biff and Happy, so they desert him and go off with two girls they have picked up.

Willy, having borrowed more money than usual from Charley in order to pay his insurance premium, returns alone to Brooklyn. He now appears to his family to have become completely insane, meticulously planting rows of seeds by night in his overshadowed garden. When the boys return with a shamefaced peace-offering of flowers for Linda she shows them Willy as the ruin he has become. Once again, in spite of an attempt at mutual understanding Willy and Biff have their final bitter disagreement. The family go into the house leaving Willy alone. He now resolves to end his life in a way that will benefit Biff, and getting into his car drives out in the night towards certain death.

The play ends with a short scene which Miller calls the Requiem in which Linda, Biff, Happy and Charley make a series of stylised comments upon Willy's life and death.

3.2 DETAILED SYNOPSIS AND COMMENTARY

The two acts can be divided into a number of shorter sequences. These are sometimes linked through timeswitches. A change from one sequence to the next, whether there is a timeswitch or not, is usually signalled by a light change, music or other sound-effect. There is no lowering of the main curtain between the sequences. In fact the general practice today is for there to be no main curtain at all. If any alteration in the setting is required at the change from one sequence to another, it usually entails no more than a few small pieces of furniture being moved on or off the stage by members of the cast in the course of the action.

There are plenty of clues within the dialogue of the play as to its *chronology* (see Section 2). The 'public action' takes place through the last twenty-four hours in Willy's life in the year 1948. Inside Willy's mind the 'private action' takes place in 'remembered time' which is usually round about the year in which Biff failed his mathematics examination and gave up the idea of going to university. Since this occurred seventeen years ago then the year of crisis is 1931, but some of Willy's memories are from farther back in time.

Each sequence has been given a number within its act, and to make the pattern of action clear there will always be indications of time and location.

Act I   Sequence 1   **Time:**   Present (night)
                              Location: Brooklyn (Main bedroom)

Summary
The atmosphere of the play is established by music of the flute. Then as the light increases the audience see the salesman's house surrounded by towering apartment blocks. The light increases and Willy is seen coming in, bent under the weight of his heavy sample cases. As he lets himself into the house, he disturbs Linda, who is not expecting him and fears that something has gone wrong. He tells her that he is not ill but is 'tired to the death' and was unable to reach his destination in New England because he suddenly lost his ability to keep control of the car. He kept forgetting that he was driving and found that the car was suddenly going off the road at sixty miles an hour. Frightened by this, he turned round and came home driving as slowly as possible. Linda is distressed but does not seem to be altogether surprised. She suggests that he must ask his employer for a job in New York so that he will not have to travel any more. Willy demurs at this because of his pride in himself as the 'New England man' but he gives in and agrees to go and see his boss on the following day.

Willy and Linda begin to talk about their sons, Biff and Happy. Linda is very pleased to have them both together on a visit, but she chides Willy for criticising Biff as soon as he met him off the train. Willy is generally dissatisfied with Biff for not settling into a regular job like his brother.

Willy seems to be generally touchy and aggressive, venting some of his anger on the building developers who have spoilt the rural character of the neighbourhood by cutting down the trees and building big apartment blocks which overshadow his garden so that he cannot grow either vegetables or flowers.

His raised voice disturbs the young men sleeping in the next room. Willy goes downstairs to the kitchen daydreaming about the happy past. (Biff and Happy are awake and listening as the lights begin to fade on the main bedroom and come on in theirs. This is an 'overlap' between the two sequences.)

Commentary
The early scenes of any play must carry the burden of *exposition*. That is to say, they have to give the audience some indication of the *atmosphere* and *general mood* of the play and also provide information about the *characters* and the *relationships* between them.

The atmosphere is partially suggested by the music. The function of setting, costume, lights and music will be discussed later, but it is worth noting that the rather strange atmosphere suggested by the flute does not seem to fit with the entrance of a rather ordinary elderly salesman with his sample cases. This apparent contradiction is, of course, intentional, although the audience will not realise it yet. Above all, an opening scene is expected to contain information about *time* and *place*. Time of day is established by the general darkness at the beginning of the play and by the fact that all the characters in this scene except Willy are in bed.

In the course of this first short scene, we are not only introduced to two of the central characters but are also given a great deal of information about them. A careful reading of the scene would provide the following list, which is by no means complete.

The name of the principal character
The name of his wife
The make of car he drives
The name of the place where he turned round to come back home
The profession of the principal character
The name of the company that employs him
The name of his present boss
The names of his sons
The kind of cheese he likes to eat

The name of the make of car he was driving in 1928
The colour of that car

(Read through other early scenes to find out what other information is given.)

Not all these facts are of equal importance for the understanding of the play. At this stage, the audience have no reason to know that the red Chevrolet is of more significance than the Studebaker, but the very fact that the audience are receiving this detailed information gives them the impression of overhearing a real conversation. Also, they absorb this necessary information without any effort at all because they are interested in the characters and are beginning to make judgements about them.

It is obvious from the dialogue, even to an audience that has not read the introductory stage direction in the printed version, that Linda loves Willy very deeply. It is also clear that at this moment in their lives, at least, she is the wiser of the two. Although alarmed she is not altogether surprised by his sudden return and seems to be prepared for bad news ('You didn't smash the car, did you?'). This together with her later lines when she begs him to go and ask Howard for a job in New York are examples of the kind of line often written into an opening scene to raise expectation and to point forward to the further development of the story. This interview with Howard will not take place until the play is approaching its end, but the audience have already been made aware of its importance in Willy's life.

It is not easy for the audience to begin to assess Willy's character at their first sight of him because he is in an unusual state of mind, but some characteristics stand out. He is proud of his professional skills ('I'm the New England man. I'm vital in New England.'). He tends to be overbearing towards Linda ('I don't want a change! I want Swiss cheese. Why am I always being contradicted?'). Yet he seems to love Linda very much ('You're not worried about me, are you, sweetheart?'). His behaviour is certainly not quite normal. His inability to concentrate on driving his car may well be symptomatic of a much deeper distress. The audience begin to wonder what is wrong so they watch him closely. His expression of love for Linda betrays his insecurity ('You're my foundation and my support, Linda.'). One aspect of his behaviour definitely verges on the abnormal. He frequently expresses himself violently ('Biff is a lazy bum!'). He shouts this and then almost immediately, in a more normal tone of voice, he contradicts himself ('There's one thing about Biff – he's not lazy.').

Towards the end of this sequence the audience are prepared for the use of the timeswitch technique.

LINDA And Willy – if it's warm Sunday we'll drive in the country. And we'll open the windshield, and take lunch.

WILLY   No, the windshield's don't open on the new cars.
LINDA   But you opened it today.
WILLY   Me? I didn't. (*He stops*) Now isn't that peculiar! Isn't that a remarkable – (*He breaks off in amazement and fright as the flute is heard distantly.*)
LINDA   What, darling?
WILLY   That is the most remarkable thing.
LINDA   What dear?
WILLY   I was thinking of the Chevvy. (*Slight pause*) Nineteen twenty-eight . . . when I had that red Chevvy – (*Breaks off*) That's funny – I coulda sworn I was driving that Chevvy today.

The sound of the flute reminds the audience that Willy is describing a very unusual experience. It is at moments like this throughout the play that the *realistic* and the *poetic* elements meet and blend. Willy is, of course, telling Linda what it feels like to experience a timeswitch. The great irony is that neither of them fully understands what he is talking about.

The dialogue just quoted has been foreshadowed by an earlier speech:

WILLY   (*with wonder*) I was driving along, you understand? And I was fine. I was even observing the scenery. You can imagine, me looking at scenery, on the road every week of my life. But it's so beautiful up there, Linda, the trees are so thick, and the sun is warm. I opened the windshield and just let the warm air bathe over me. And then all of a sudden I'm going 'off the road'. (*He presses two fingers against his eyes.*) I have such thoughts, I have such strange thoughts.

This is a brilliantly economical way of introducing an original technical device.

The first real timeswitch within the play begins as Willy goes out of the bedroom remembering the red Chevrolet and the way Biff used to Simonize it. Biff and Happy are already in the action and are beginning to be visible, sitting up in their beds next door. They have been awakened by Willy's speech about the apartment houses, delivered in a loud voice.

Act I   Sequence 2   **Time:**   Present (night)
                                 Location: Brooklyn (Boys' bedroom)

Summary
This sequence introduces an important component of the plot – Biff's

decision to approach his old employer, Bill Oliver, for money to buy a ranch. (This project becomes modified later in the play, and there is just a hint that Biff's relationship with Oliver is somewhat ambiguous.) The rest of the scene serves to outline the contrasting characters of the two sons. Happy is a moderately successful business man who has moved out from the Loman family home into his own bachelor apartment where he leads a pleasure-loving existence. Biff tells his brother that although he enjoys working on the ranches of the West every spring he gets the feeling that he is wasting his time doing so when he should be building a secure future for himself. The sons discuss what is happening to their father. Happy expresses concern about Willy, mainly because he has been nervous about his father's erratic driving and embarrassed by his habit of muttering to himself in public but he has done very little about it except to pay for Willy to take a vacation in Florida. Biff's reaction to overhearing Willy muttering as he goes downstairs past the bedroom is not one of pity but of contemptuous anger. He seems to be very sorry for Linda but dismisses Willy as 'selfish and stupid'.

Commentary
It is significant that the audience first see the Loman brothers apart from their parents in their own bedroom, just after they have met again after a long separation. This gives them the chance to discuss their father quite frankly and to talk about their relationships with women more openly than they could in Linda's presence. Their attitude to the opposite sex, especially as expressed by Happy, would be open to strong criticism today, but is fairly typical of its own time. The playwright is establishing a group of related themes – to be developed later in the play. The following piece of dialogue is typical in that it introduces a *general theme* (sexual relationships) and follows it immediately by applying it to one particular character – in this instance it is Biff.

> BIFF   Remember that big Betsy something – what the hell was her name – over on Bushwick Avenue?
> HAPPY   (*combing his hair*) With the collie dog?
> BIFF   That's the one. I got you in there, remember?
> HAPPY   Yeah, that was my first time – I think. Boy, there was a pig! (*They laugh, almost crudely.*) You taught me everything I know about women. Don't forget that.
> BIFF   I bet you forgot how bashful you used to be. Especially with girls.
> HAPPY   Oh, I still am, Biff.
> BIFF   Oh, go on.
> HAPPY   I just control it, that's all. I think I got less bashful and

you got more so. What happened, Biff? Where's the old humour, the old confidence? (*He shakes Biff's knee. Biff gets up and moves restlessly about the room.*) What's the matter?

BIFF   Why does Dad mock me all the time?

This establishes the closeness and mutual affection between the brothers, but it indicates, too, that Biff has changed. He has become bashful with women while Happy has become more brash. It is also implied that the change in Biff may be connected with his altered relationship with Willy, and that this secret is strictly between Willy and Biff because neither Linda nor Happy, although aware of the tension between Biff and his father, knows the cause. Another minor but significant component of the plot is being established: the connection, in the minds of the audience, between the interest that the Loman brothers have always had in sporting matters and Biff's desire to settle down into a proper business venture. Their relationship with Bill Oliver is not yet made clear, but it will have an important effect on Willy's future.

The transition into the next sequence is slow and with considerable overlap. Willy is heard talking in the kitchen. He now imagines himself to be back in the Brooklyn he knew in the happy past, around the year 1928. He sees his sons as high school boys busily cleaning his car – the red Chevrolet already mentioned. Upstairs in their bedroom, the grown-up Happy and Biff finish their conversation and go back to bed. In the kitchen, the light change begins as Willy opens the refrigerator to take out a bottle of milk. Simultaneously, to the accompaniment of music, the scene changes. The apartment blocks disappear, the Loman house and garden become sunlit and covered with leaves.

Act I   Sequence 3   **Time:** Past (day)

Location: Brooklyn (house and garden)

Summary
Willy has just returned, like a conquering hero, from one of his business trips. Biff has just been made football captain and is basking in the glory of the admiration of his classmates, male and female. A sour note is struck by Bernard, the earnest bespectacled student from next door who comes to warn Biff that he must study his mathematics if he hopes to go to university. Biff refuses Bernard's help and seems to expect to be able to graduate on personality alone. Willy supports him and tells the boys that Bernard, although a better student than Biff, will never succeed as well in the business world because he will never be 'as well liked'. In this, according to Willy, Bernard resembles his father, Charley, a business man and a friend of Willy's. Willy

confides to his sons that he intends to set up his own business so that
he will be 'bigger' than Charley someday.

Willy and Linda begin to calculate how much Willy has earned and
to set it against the amount they owe. It becomes obvious that they
are not very prosperous and cannot always meet every debt. Linda
tells Willy that he is doing very well, but he confesses to her that he
thinks he lacks self-confidence. To encourage him she tells him that
he is the handsomest man in the world and that he is idolised by his
children. Willy's next speech leads into the following sequence
through a timeswitch.

Commentary
During the transition from the previous sequence, Willy is heard
warning Biff against taking too much interest in girls while he is still
quite young. This is ironic both in the light of the conversation between the grown-up brothers and also of what is soon to be revealed.
Exposition of *time* and *place* is developed in greater detail by
reference to the Chevrolet car and the way in which the boys were
expected to polish it until it shone, the hammock Willy intends to buy
to swing between the two elm trees and the gift that he brings the
boys – a punch-bag bearing the signature of Gene Tunney, the then
undefeated heavyweight boxing champion of the world. In this
sequence, the audience see for the first time the younger Willy,
self-confident vigorous and optimistic, expounding his philosophy of
success through being well-liked. Although he is scornful of the
hard-working and intelligent Bernard and teaches his sons to take the
same attitude, he is already secretly aware that he is not being as
successful as he would wish.

The next timeswitch is the first to bring about a change of location.

Act I   Sequence 4   **Time:**   Past (night)
                                Location: Boston (hotel bedroom)

Summary
This sequence establishes that Willy is carrying on an affair with the
Woman who works for one of his customers in Boston. She is 'quite
proper looking' and of Willy's age. She is fond of him and shares his
slightly vulgar sense of humour. There is no grand passion about the
relationship and she is in no way a rival to Linda.

Commentary
This is another economical scene establishing just what is necessary
and no more. Any attempt to deepen the character of the Woman
would have been a mistake. (She is not even given a name.) The
sequence is inserted in the play at this particular moment to give the

audience a piece of information about Willy which is not known to the other characters at this time. It has its maximum dramatic effect because Willy guiltily remembers his mistress at the very moment in which he feels affection towards his wife. (' . . . on the road I want to grab you sometimes and just kiss the life outa you.')

The timeswitch is established by sound (music and the Woman's laughter) and by lights (involving the use of a transparency in the wall of the set). There is also an *ambivalent phrase* in the dialogue. Willy tells Linda, 'There's so much I want to make for – ' he is using the word 'make' here in its ordinary sense of 'making money' or things for the house, so that the sentence, if completed, would have been – 'there's so much I want to make for you.' But the reply comes not from Linda, but from the Woman who uses the same word with a different meaning. Finishing his sentence for him she says, 'Me? You didn't make me, Willy. I picked you.' In this context, the word 'make' is a slang term meaning 'to get acquainted with a person', usually for the purposes of sexual adventure.

There is an ironic echo in the transition to Sequence 5. The Woman's laughter blends with Linda's. Willy's memory has only lasted long enough for Linda to finish her sentence and to start mending her stockings.

Act I Sequence 5	**Time:** Past (day)
	Location: Brooklyn (kitchen)

Summary
The return to Brooklyn is brought about by the Woman disappearing into darkness as Willy remembers his guilt and covers it by going into a rage over Linda mending stockings. (He always gives the Woman stockings as a present.)

By now, Biff is causing Willy mounting anxiety by neglecting to study for an approaching examination which he must pass if he is to graduate. He is getting out of hand generally, terrorising the girls by his roughness, stealing from the school sports store and driving the car without a licence. Linda is worried about Biff's future but Willy defends him ('You want him to be a worm like *Bernard*? He's got spirit, personality . . . ') Privately, though, Willy is beginning to feel worried about him.

Commentary
On the return to Brooklyn after the timeswitch it appears that there has been no break in the continuity but the speeches given to Bernard and Linda suggest that time is passing. The important Regents examination is getting uncomfortably near. Mr Birnbaum, the mathematics teacher, is mentioned. He remains offstage throughout the play, but his dislike of Biff will be a contributory factor in Willy's

downfall. The sequence is very short and the dialogue moves quickly and becomes less *realistic*. At one point the Woman's laughter is heard when both Linda and Bernard are pressing Willy to do something about Biff. Willy shouts, 'Shut up!' as much at the Woman, who is still in his mind, as at the two people who are actually present.

The action returns to the present as Linda and Bernard go off, leaving Willy alone. The lights change and the leaves fade away. The adult Happy comes downstairs in his pyjamas to persuade Willy to return to bed.

Act I   Sequence 6   **Time:**   Present (night)
                                           Location: Brooklyn (kitchen)

Summary
Willy tells Happy he regrets that he did not go to Alaska with his brother Ben who subsequently made a fortune in diamonds. Happy offers to support Willy in retirement but Willy points out that he might be reluctant to sacrifice his own expensive lifestyle. They are joined by Charley who signals Happy to leave them alone. He has been disturbed by Willy's return and has come round to offer help if needed. He brings a note of normality with him and compliments Willy on the skill he has shown in putting up a new ceiling in the house, but Willy remains aggressive towards him.

Commentary
This sequence is short but the general tempo is reduced by the entrance of the slow-speaking, laconic Charley, who introduces a note of everyday commonsense. The audience learn that Willy has practical skills but does not seem to be willing to talk about them.

Act I   Sequence 7   **Time:**   Present (night)
                                           Location: Brooklyn (kitchen)

Summary
For the first time in the play, the 'public world' which Willy inhabits with other people becomes confused with the private world of his memory and imagination. He tries to live in both worlds at once as he plays cards with Charley while carrying on a conversation with the ghost of his elder brother Ben. The slight tendency towards melodrama in this scene is offset by the comedy of Charley's growing bewilderment and irritation.

Commentary

There are some parallels between this sequence and the scene in Shakespeare's *Macbeth* when the ghost of Banquo appears at the feast. The stage direction at the beginning of this sequence suggests that Willy 'conjures up' Ben simply by speaking to him. Ben is an important character, different from every other character in the play. Having appeared, he stays in one place outside the imagined line of the kitchen wall. The next sequence begins when Willy walks through this line into the past to meet Ben on the day that he paid his visit to Brooklyn.

Act I   Sequence 8   **Time:** Past (day)
                           Location: Brooklyn (garden and house)

Summary

Willy proudly introduces his elder brother to his wife and family. He and Ben exchange memories of their father, a travelling craftsman and inventor who made flutes and sold them throughout the United States from east to west. Linda is both suspicious and frightened of Ben. She disapproves of him, most of all for challenging Biff to a fight and then using unfair methods to defeat him. Ben simply laughs and says that he is teaching Biff 'never to fight fair with a stranger'. Willy sends the boys to steal building equipment from the adjacent site where the apartment blocks are being erected. The watchman chases the boys away much to Willy's amusement.

Left alone with Ben at the end of the sequence, Willy asks his advice on the upbringing of Biff and Happy. Ben's answer is typical – 'William, when I walked into the jungle, I was seventeen. When I walked out I was twenty-one. And, by God, I was rich!'

Commentary

It gradually becomes clear that Miller intends the flute music to be connected in some way with the origins of the Loman family and the pioneering days of the American West. Both Ben and Willy are descendants of a remarkable man who combined many talents. They have developed differently, with Ben retaining more of his father's characteristics than Willy. Ben is the last major character to be presented to the audience and he brings a strange atmosphere with him whenever he appears.

The exposition is now almost complete in that all the principal characters are clearly outlined and the unusual narration technique (the timeswitch) has been established, but the *plot* has been scarcely developed as yet. That has to wait until the second act. On the exit of Ben a light change leads into the last sequence of Act 1.

24

Act 1 Sequence 9

Time: Present (night)
Location: Brooklyn (garden and house)

Summary
Linda comes downstairs to the kitchen in her dressing-gown. She looks for Willy and finds him in the garden. She tries to persuade him to return to bed, but he is still thinking about Ben and the diamond watch-fob that his brother gave him. In spite of being in his slippers he insists on going for a walk. Linda is joined first by Biff and then by Happy and she is very angry with them both for neglecting their father in his time of need. She reveals to them that Willy is now exhausted and unable to find new business for the firm. Because he is not getting results his salary has been stopped so that he is now working for commission only, just like a beginner. Sometimes he travels a long way and works hard and still earns nothing at all. Although Willy has not told her, she has discovered that he is borrowing money from Charley in order to pretend that he is still on salary. Once again, she challenges Biff to tell her why it is that he and Willy can never agree. Biff say that Willy is a fake but refuses to tell her why he thinks so. Nevertheless, he is willing to stay in New York in order to be able to help her financially.

Linda then tells them that Willy has been trying to kill himself and is still likely to do so. Biff is shocked at this and tells Linda that, much as he dislikes the whole of the world of business, he will try to make good for her sake. When Willy returns there is immediate friction between him and Biff which lasts until he is told of the boys' plan to go to New York to ask for financial backing for Bill Oliver. This is not for a ranch, as originally intended, but for a scheme to sell Oliver's sports goods through a series of public displays of athletic skills by Biff and Happy as the 'Loman Brothers'. This ideas pleases and excites Willy, but even so he tries to dominate their plans thus straining Biff's patience.

The first act ends quietly with Linda humming a lullaby to Willy as he tries to go to sleep, remembering Biff as the hero of the championship football game.

Commentary
This final sequence serves to tie Act 1 together. Apart from the revelations made by Linda and the elaboration of the idea to be sold to Bill Oliver, the sequence contains very little new information for the audience, but the emotional tone is raised considerably by Linda's denunciation of her sons for their ingratitude. There is one moment when the truth about Willy's relationship with the Woman seems about to slip out, but the moment passes. That revelation will be kept until later.

At the end of the Act, Biff accepts responsibility for his father by removing the rubber tube which Willy has fitted as a suicide device to the gas heater. Willy assures Linda that everything will be all right and gazes up at the moon between the apartment blocks as the lights fade for the end of the first act.

Act II   Sequence 1   **Time:**   Present (day)
                              Location: Brooklyn (kitchen)

Summary
Willy and Linda are at breakfast. The atmosphere is brisk and hopeful. The language is realistic with constant reference to domestic details. Willy and Linda both appear to be confident that Biff will be able to persuade Bill Oliver to back his project and that Willy himself will succeed in getting his job in New York with the Wagner company. Willy even begins to plan for a future in which both the sons will have married and moved away. He begins to think of planning and building two guest houses for them to stay in when they visit. Linda, more practically, reminds Willy to ask for an advance from Howard Wagner as soon as he has been given the job because they have outstanding debts, including Willy's life insurance premium and the last payment on the mortgage on the house. As Willy is going, Linda tells him that the boys have invited him to join them for a meal at a restaurant in New York that evening.

Commentary
For all the rapid tempo and superficial hopefulness of this sequence, it contains many ironical lines. There is the reference to the life insurance and the final payment on the mortgage, also Willy's pathetic hope that Biff would take over the house and raise a family. Even at this moment of hope, Willy is reminded of his unfaithfulness when Linda kisses him goodbye, carrying a stocking that she has been mending.

The first sequence is linked to the next through a telephone call which is from Biff in New York. He tells Linda that he is at Bill Oliver's office but has not yet been able to see him. She tells him that Willy has just left home in high spirits and she asks Biff to be kind to his father when they meet.

During this speech Howard Wagner enters wheeling the table with the recorder on it. The lights cross-fade from the kitchen to left forestage which becomes Howard's office.

Act II   Sequence 2   **Time:** Present (day)
                             Location: New York (Howard Wagner's
                                               office)

Summary
At first, Howard is deeply absorbed in listening to the voices of his
family from his tape recorder so that he does not notice Willy's
arrival. When Willy finally gets his attention, he listens courteously,
but firmly refuses to give Willy a job in the New York office. When
Willy points out that he has been working for the Wagner company
since before Howard was born, Howard replies that while he
appreciates Willy's long service there is simply no place for him.
Willy then tells Howard how he refused a chance to go to Alaska at
the time of the gold rush, because he met an old salesman called
Dave Singleman who impressed him so much that he decided that
'selling was the greatest career a man could want'. Howard remains
unimpressed and Willy becomes desperate and begins to shout at him
so that Howard decides to leave him alone for a while so that he can
recover himself.
    Alone, Willy imagines that he can see Frank Wagner, the founder
of the company and Howard's father, sitting at the desk. He leans
over to speak to him and inadvertently switches on the recorder and
does not know how to stop it. Willy panics and calls for Howard who,
when he returns, loses patience with Willy and tells him that he can
no longer work for the Wagner company.

Commentary
The plot is beginning to unfold and the pace increases. From now on,
the sequence-changes tend to be very simple and swift.
    The long-heralded interview between Willy and his boss might
have been expected to be very dramatic, with Howard depicted as a
hard business man, but this sequence has a great deal of comedy in it.
Howard appears to be a well-meaning, if somewhat lazy and self-
centred young man, unlikely to be willing to fire Willy until virtually
forced to do so. The high point of the scene is Willy's long speech
about Dave Singleman, who is one of the important off-stage
characters like Bill Oliver and Mr Birnbaum, who influence Willy's
destiny but are never seen by the audience. Willy's very brief speech
to Frank Wagner can scarcely be classified as a timeswitch. Frank
never speaks to Willy and never completely materialises. (The
obvious reason for this is that it would be pointless to employ an actor
for so short an appearance!)

Act II   Sequence 3   **Time:**   Past (day)
                                   Location: Brooklyn (garden and house)

Summary
Howard goes off, wheeling the table with the tape recorder on it.
Willy stands still, confused and exhausted. He hears Ben's music
approaching. Ben himself appears and takes up the same position
that he held on his first entrance, just outside the wall of the house.
He tells Willy that he is just looking in on his way back from Alaska,
where he has been buying timberland.
  Willy confesses that he is very unhappy about the future. Ben
immediately offers him the job of managing his new property in
Alaska. Willy is ready to accept this but Linda immediately opposes
the idea. She tells Ben that Willy is doing so well in New England for
the Wagner company that Wagner senior has offered to make him a
member of the firm. When Ben challenges Willy to explain exactly
what he thinks he is building with the Wagner company, Willy has
no answer until Linda reminds him of his own story about Dave
Singleman. Ben becomes impatient and is about to depart, but at this
point the young Biff makes a triumphal entrance with Happy and
Bernard, on his way to lead his team in the game for the All-
Scholastic Championship of the City of New York. Willy, believing
that Biff is set to become another Dave Singleman, proudly calls
Ben's attention to Biff as a living proof that 'a man can end up with
diamonds on the basis of being liked!'
  Ben withdraws. Willy and his sons, together with the faithful
Bernard set out for the game in a mood of high elation, which is spoilt
by Charley, the solemn-faced humorist, pretending not to know what
the excitement is all about. He even pretends not to know the
difference between baseball and football. Willy fiercely resents his
belittlement of the occasion and challenges him to a fist fight.

Commentary
The timeswitch is established very simply by Howard's exit and
reinforced by the use of Ben's music. The action of the sequence is
made up from the contrasting memories that fill Willy's mind on his
way to Charley's office on the afternoon of the last day of his life. He
recalls his crucial and, as it now appears, fatal decision to remain with
the Wagner company instead of going to Alaska. The audience are
now given a different view of the circumstances surrounding that
decision.
  It has become obvious in the previous sequence that Willy consistently exaggerated his success with the Wagner company. Linda has
always believed what he told her, including the unlikely offer of a
partnership by Wagner senior. This, quite apart from her dislike of
Ben, makes her strongly oppose any suggestion of moving to Alaska.

Yet Willy still believes in his philosophy of success through being well-liked and he remembers with pride the glory of Biff's success at Ebbets Field and especially the touchdown by his son.

This memory turns sour as he remembers how Charley made unfeeling jokes on what to him was an occasion of solemn splendour. Behind all this, the feeling of defeat remains. Willy knows that now that he has no job, he will have to borrow more than ever from Charley with no hope of repayment. He arrives at Charley's office in an aggressive mood which will persist when he comes out of timeswitch into the present.

Act II   Sequence 4   **Time:** Present (day)
                           Location: New York (Charley's office)

Summary
Bernard is waiting to see his father before going to Washington where, as a rising young lawyer, he will be pleading a case before the Supreme Court. He asks Willy to tell him how it was that Biff never went to university, because he could have caught up with maths in summer school. He knows that Biff went to Boston to see Willy and he wonders what happened there. Willy becomes angry and refuses to discuss the matter further. After Bernard has gone, Willy asks Charley for another loan, as he calls it, and remembers to add the extra money for the life insurance. Once more, Charley offers Willy a regular job which he refuses.

Throughout the entire interview Willy is offensive, but at the end of it he realises that he is jealous of Charley. Yet, he also has come to realise that Charley is his only friend.

Commentary
The dream of success has been followed by the realisation of failure. Bernard, whom Willy had always despised, has now become a very successful attorney and is married with two children of his own. The fact that Bernard is a family man is hurtful to Willy in the light of his dreams for his sons at the beginning of the act.

Act II   Sequence 5   **Time:** Present (evening)
                           Location: New York (restaurant)

Summary
The sequences are linked by a sudden blackout and raucous music. Stanley, the waiter, and Happy come in with tables and chairs. Happy is enjoying the task of ordering a meal for his father and brother. While he is doing so, Miss Forsythe, an attractive and lavishly dressed young woman comes in. Happy immediately turns his charm on her and persuades her not only to join them but to call

up a friend for Biff. Meanwhile, Biff tells Happy that he waited for six hours to see Bill Oliver who, when he at last came out of his office, walked past him without recognition. While Miss Forsythe is out making the phone call, Biff tells Happy he has realised that he has been deceiving himself into believing that he was a salesman for Oliver, when in fact his position was much less important. Worse than that, when he was left alone he had gone into Oliver's empty office and taken his fountain pen. He cannot understand why he committed this pointless theft and he wants Happy to help him to explain the affair to Willy. Happy thinks that this will be difficult and suggests that they concoct a story for Willy which will please him for the time being. While they are discussing this, Willy comes in. Before Biff can prepare Willy to hear the truth, Willy announces that he has been fired by Howard and is relying on Biff to give him some good news to tell Linda.

This places Biff at a disadvantage because Happy is quite prepared to invent good news for Willy's benefit to keep the peace for the time being. Biff is forced to consent to a lie. Willy takes charge of the conversation, making it impossible for Biff to tell the truth. Biff turns to Happy and exclaims, 'I can't talk to him!'

This speech is the cue for the next timeswitch. There is a single jarring trumpet note and the house behind them lights up with the green leaves establishing the past.

Act II   Sequence 6   **Time:**   Past (night)
                                   Location: Brooklyn (exterior of house)

Summary
The young Bernard rushes in knocking at the door and calling urgently for Linda. He tells her that Biff has failed his final mathematics examination and that Mr Birnbaum is refusing to graduate him. He also tells her that Biff has gone to Boston to find Willy to see if he can help him. Linda is very sorry for Biff but hopes that Willy will return and talk to Mr Birnbaum.

Commentary
This short, rapid sequence is played simultaneously behind the men in the restaurant. In the meantime, Biff has been trying to explain exactly what happened in Bill Oliver's office. He does not realise that Willy, who is still in a state of shock from having been sacked by Howard, regards Biff's announcement as yet another defeat for the Loman family. It reminds him of the fateful night when the young Biff came to him in Boston having failed maths.

A simple adjustment of light is enough to bring the action out of the timeswitch.

Act II   Sequence 7   **Time:**   Present (evening)
                                        Location: New York (restaurant)

Summary
Willy's mind continues to fluctuate between past and present. Almost
simultaneously he hears his telephone ring in Boston and the page
calling his name as the young Biff tries to find him. Meanwhile, in the
restaurant, the adult Biff is desperately trying to convince him that
there is no point in trying to see Bill Oliver again. Failing to
understand what it is that Biff is trying to tell him, Willy comes to the
conclusion that Biff is trying to spite him. Even as he accuses Biff, he
hears the Woman laugh in Boston. Willy strikes Biff. Happy manages
to separate the two men just as Miss Forsythe returns with her friend.
Biff controls himself and introduces Willy. He almost persuades him
to join them in a drink, but Willy hears the Woman's voice once
more. Now completely confused as to his whereabouts, he mutters
something about 'opening the door'. This is in fact addressed to the
Woman in Boston, but Biff thinking that his father is drunk or ill
leads him off in the direction of the restaurant washroom.
    There follows a brief but fierce argument between Biff and Happy,
keeping their voices low because of the girls. Biff goes out in a rage
but Happy is unconcerned. He calmly and cheerfully takes the girls
out to catch up with Biff with the intention of spending the rest of the
evening together. One of the girls asks about Willy, but Happy says,
'No, that's not my father. He's just a guy.'

Commentary
This is a very complex sequence, difficult to describe, but dramatically very effective. It has been very carefully prepared for. The
audience are by now willing to accept the use of the timeswitch in a
variety of ways. It is a prelude to the revelation which will occur in the
following sequence, although many of the audience will already have
guessed what is about to be disclosed.

Act II   Sequence 8   **Time:**   Past (night)
                                        Location: Boston (hotel bedroom)

Summary
Willy and the Woman are together in the hotel bedroom when they
are disturbed by the young Biff. Willy sends the Woman into the
bathroom and admits Biff, who tells him what has happened,
blaming Mr Birnbaum for being prejudiced against him because Biff
once mocked him in front of the class. Willy agrees to return with Biff
immediately but the Woman emerges from the bathroom. Willy tries
to make Biff accept a rather thin cover story but Biff is angry and
hurt. For the first time in his life he calls his father a 'phoney little

fake'. Biff goes out rapidly although Willy tries to order him to come back. Once again, there is an ambiguous linking speech. Willy shouts to Biff 'I gave you an order' but he finds himself back in the restaurant shouting at Stanley the waiter.

Commentary
The timeswitch from New York to Boston is made by Stanley, the waiter, calling indignantly after Happy, 'Mr Loman! Mr Loman!' As the lights change, his voice could well be that of the hotel page calling for Willy. The audience are prepared for the revelation of Willy's guilty secret by a series of *warning sounds*, beginning with the trumpet note in Sequence 6 and including Bernard's frantic knocking on Linda's door, Willy's phone bell ringing in Boston and the voice of the Woman. All these serve to heighten the tension and to increase the feeling of approaching disaster.

The revelation itself when it comes is scarcely surprising, but the playwright is not aiming at *melodrama*. In the nineteenth century such a confrontation between a guilty father and his son would have been made into a moment of high drama. In the *social drama* of Ibsen the fact of Willy's relationship with the Woman would have been treated as a 'family secret' and its revelation might well have been the climax of the play. In this play the true climax comes later when Willy finally decides to die for Biff's sake. Strangely enough, the sequence contains some moments of comedy such as Biff's impersonation of Mr Birnbaum and the Woman's verbal clowning early in the scene. These serve to heighten the real pathos and the extra shock for Biff when he discovers that the Woman has been given the stockings that he thinks should be Linda's.

Act II   Sequence 9   **Time:** Present (evening)
                                 Location: New York (restaurant)

Summary
Stanley, the waiter, is sympathetic in his handling of Willy, whom he regards as an elderly drunk who has been ditched by the young people. Willy asks him where he can buy seeds. Stanley tells him and Willy goes out. Stanley assisted by another waiter, removes the tables and chairs.

Commentary
This very short sequence maintains the emotional tension very well because of the unsolicited kindness of the young waiter and Willy's blind instinctive urge to plant seeds for the future.

(At this point, the flow of sequences is halted. The light fades on the empty stage and there is a long pause with the sound of the flute coming over, indicating the passage of time, during which Willy has made his way home, having bought packets of seed on the way while Biff and Happy have been enjoying themselves on the town with the girls.)

Act II   Sequence 10

Time: Present (night)
Location: Brooklyn (house and garden)

Summary
Biff and Happy return home still slightly under the influence of drink and the excitement of the evening out but also feeling increasingly guilty. They have brought a present of flowers for their mother. Linda is blazing with anger. She calls their attention to Willy who is in the garden by himself planting his seeds. From their point of view, he is alone, but muttering audibly to himself.

Commentary
This sequence is short but very powerful. After an almost comic beginning when the boys enter almost stealthily with their ridiculous bunch of flowers, the tension rises with their confrontation with Linda's superb anger and freezes into extreme pathos at the spectacle of Willy in what seems to them to be a state of mental collapse.

Act II   Sequence 11

Time: Present (night)
Location: Brooklyn (garden)

Summary
Willy comes into view, planting seeds in the dark by the light of a flashlight. He is quite unaware that his behaviour might seem strange to his family. He is preoccupied with thoughts of suicide. These have been in his mind for a long time but he is still uncertain as to whether it will work out in the way he hopes. For the last time in his life, he turns to Ben for advice, seeming to take it for granted that Ben will appear when he needs him. Willy explains that he knows Linda has suffered and deserves whatever comfort she can buy with the $20,000 she will receive when Willy dies. Ben expresses doubts. He points out that the company may repudiate the policy. He also says that suicide is considered to be the act of a coward, but Willy argues that he has worked hard to pay the premiums and it takes courage to kill oneself. He feels that there is great certainty to be derived from a large sum of money like $20,000. It is tangible and powerful 'like a diamond'. Above all Willy wants Biff to stop hating and despising him. He believes that his funeral will be very impressive, with salesmen coming from all over New England, so that Biff will at last be forced to realise how well known and well liked his father was.
    When Ben says that Biff will still call Willy a coward and continue to hate him in spite of all this, Willy becomes desperate and expresses

his great longing for the happy times in the past, when he still had a future and his boys were young and näive enough to trust and idolise him.

Biff is heard approaching. Ben asks for time to think about the proposition and retires into the darkness.

Commentary
This compressed and intense sequence brilliantly solves the technical problem facing the playwright at this point. In the previous sequence there has been the powerful confrontation between Linda and her sons, culminating in her revelation that Willy now seems to be out of his mind. During this, Willy is off-stage. (This gives the leading actor a short but useful rest between the complex emotional demands of the restaurant scenes and the intensity of the final sequences.)

The writer's problem is to find a way for the audience to know what Willy is thinking about as he plants his seeds, apparently alone in the garden. The solution is to use the character of Ben, evoked by Willy, not in his usual flamboyant persona but rather as the voice of caution and reason. This means that the audience can be fully informed about Willy's motives for suicide.

The sequence is filled with ironies. It is ironical that Willy's last act before killing himself should be to plant seeds in an overshadowed garden where nothing will grow any more. Behind that is the symbolic irony in the fact that most of Willy's working life had been spent in 'spreading seed upon stony ground'. It also arises from the fact that Willy's *seed*, in the sense of his descendants, will never become the magnificent dynasty that he has dreamed of. There is even further irony in that the terminology of business negotiation is used to help a man to decide to kill himself.

Act II   Sequence 12   **Time:**   Present (night)
                          Location: Brooklyn (garden)

Summary
Biff makes his last effort to persuade Willy to admit the truth about himself and his family. Willy persists in saying that Biff is taking this attitude simply out of spite. Even when Biff tells him that he is leaving Brooklyn for good, Willy refuses to accept any blame. Biff produces the hose from the gas heater to prove to Willy that he knows about Willy's intention to kill himself. He also confesses that he is a thief and has been in jail. Desperately, he tries to force Willy to admit that neither of them is anything other than a very ordinary man ('I am not a leader of men, Willy, and neither are you.'). His anger, together with his great sorrow, makes him break down and weep. Willy realises at last that Biff loves him. Ben appears, as he did before, just outside the kitchen. Willy has made up his mind that he must die so that Biff may inherit the $20,000 which he can use to fulfil

his early promise of magnificence. Willy goes back into the garden again to listen to the voice of Ben, who is leading him towards his death with strange cryptic promises ('The jungle is dark but full of diamonds, Willy.'). Linda calls fearfully to him, but Willy goes quickly out. There is the sound of a car starting and moving away at full speed.

Commentary
This final sequence combines and resolves the various themes within the play, bringing it towards a powerful ending through a double climax.

The last bitter confrontation between Willy and Biff is dramatically very effective because it follows a pattern of family crisis that is recognisable to most audiences. The tension which has been growing between father and son over many years erupts into a fierce quarrel, in spite of Biff's desperate attempt to avoid it. He is prepared to leave the family home for ever but wishes to part friends with Willy. Willy rejects him in a series of speeches couched in language filled with images of violence. This precipitates the first climax when Biff finds that his enduring love for Willy prevents him from hurting him any more. Like a surgeon unable to use his knife on a loved one, he breaks down and goes into the house.

At this point, a 'happy ending' would still be possible if Willy would only admit his failings and so release the family from his impossible dreams. If he could do this, then he could go into the house and come to a practical understanding with them, and, after cool discussion, he could agree to go on living modestly but in touch with reality for the remainder of his life. But he is still under the influence of Ben, who is tempting him towards suicide.

It is now Linda's turn to take up the struggle to save Willy, but she faces an invisible enemy, deeply hidden 'inside Willy's head'. Even though Willy now realises that Biff loves him, he can only respond to this love by killing himself because he is obsessed with the notion that wealth is essential for greatness. This is the final crowning irony in a play full of irony. The dialogue becomes less realistic as the end approaches and as Willy's mind begins to lose touch with reality for the last time. His final speech is spoken *elegiacally*, as a comment on his own death and begins a timeswitch back to the moment of Biff's triumph at the football game. The rest of the story is told mainly through music and other sounds which lead straight into the Requiem.

The Requiem

Summary
The sound of Willy's car blends with the music, which changes mood and finally becomes a funeral march, during which Charley and

Bernard, soberly dressed, enter and knock on the door of the house. Biff and Happy slowly descend the stairs to admit them. All four men then wait for Linda to come downstairs in full mourning carrying a small bunch of roses. The funeral party moves to the forestage, where Linda lays the roses on the grave and kneels. After a pause, the men gently try to persuade her to come home with them, but she is still dazed and uncomprehending. She cannot understand why it is that none of the salesmen who knew Willy have come to his funeral. She finds it difficult to believe that Willy is really dead and not simply away on a trip.

Biff remembers the good days when Willy used to come home and work, making improvements to the house. He suggests that more of the real Willy went into making the house better than ever went into his salesmanship, but Charley replies by making a short speech about the nature of salesmen. In his opinion, 'a salesman has got to dream'. Biff retorts that Willy had the wrong dreams and never knew who he really was. Happy fiercely denies this and the brothers almost fight each other over their father's grave.

Linda is led away by Biff, still wondering why it is that there will be no one at home in the house which is now finally paid for. The rest of the people follow them as the stage darkens and the sound of the flute is heard.

Commentary
A requiem is usually defined as a mass for the dead, that they may have peace. The five characters who stand by Willy's grave cannot be said to be praying, they are simply making comments on Willy's life. In doing so, they tell the audience more about themselves than about the man they are mourning. The language is formalised. Linda's speech is simple and sad, but carries ironic undertones.

Charley's speech about salesmen seems to be slightly out of character, but it makes a valid comment and prompts Biff to make his own shrewd and accurate judgement on his father's basic failing – 'He had the wrong dreams.' Happy remains Willy's son, blindly committed to go on making his father's mistakes all over again If he ever has a son, we feel that he will bring him up in Willy's way.

The play ends with a final symbolic comment made through the lighting and the music. The melody played on the flute, with its message of the wide open spaces of pioneering America, fades away and the grim outlines of the apartment blocks remain.

It could be argued that the story has been told completely by the end of the last sequence of the second act, but a successful performance usually has such a strong emotional impact as to make this *coda* necessary to allow the audience to return to normality with the surviving characters.

4 THEMES AND ISSUES

4.1 POLITICAL ISSUES

When *Death of a Salesman* was first produced in 1949, many people took it for granted that it had been written as an attack on American capitalism and, perhaps, on the whole American way of life. Scarcely any professional theatre critics shared this view, but Miller had acquired a reputation for radicalism with such members of the general public as had heard of him in those days. This was based mainly on his association with the Federal Theatre and the Group Theatre. He is also a Jewish intellectual and was therefore a target for political slander from the extreme right.

His previous play, *All My Sons*, has definitely radical undertones. The central character, Joe Keller, makes a fortune out of supplying the government with defective aeroplane parts during the war, thus causing the death of many American pilots. Furthermore, he evades responsibility for this and allows his partner to go to jail. In the immediate post-war period, many American families were still mourning for lost sons and it could have been said that Miller was trying to make political capital out of their resentment at those who had made money out of the war. Those who have studied Miller's work can see that *All My Sons* follows logically from the prize-winning plays he had written when he was a student. The construction and the dialogue suggest that it is modelled on the social dramas of Henrik Ibsen.

In the 1980s, it appears obvious that *Death of a Salesman* cannot be regarded as being a propaganda play. It is true that there are incidental references to sharp practice in advertising and in time-payment agreements, but these are only mentioned in passing in Act I, Sequence 3. Certainly, Willy is badly treated by his employer. After many years of faithful service he loses first his salary and then his job. His lifestyle is compared unfavourably with that of his employer. On the other hand, Howard Wagner is not a hard-hearted man and he is not dedicated to ruthless business efficiency. In the fatal interview, it is in fact Willy who forces the unfortunate outcome. Above all the Wagner company seems to be a small family firm and not the multimillion dollar monster that might appear to be a fair target for socialist criticism.

Nevertheless, in the 1950s, such was the political climate that the play was regarded by many people as an attempt to discredit American business methods which have their roots in the concepts of free enterprise and open competition. These ideas in their turn are derived from the ideals of liberty and equality which are written into the American constitution itself. Nowadays, very few people would seriously claim that *Death of a Salesman* is an anti-American play, or even anti-capitalist. It is true that some components in the collective self-image shared by most Americans are examined closely and ironically. The idea that the commercial prosperity of the United States depends upon the salesmanship of thousands of men like Willy Loman is more than slightly ridiculous, and for all the reverence that contemporary Americans may feel for the founding fathers of the republic, the play certainly seems to suggest that, while his ancestors may have been giants, the present-day American is intellectually and spiritually a very little man – like Willy Loman.

If this was indeed Miller's intention, he was writing more like a moralist than a political reformer. At the time, his intention was misunderstood in some quarters. For instance, both the play and the film version were picketed by extremist organisations and the company which produced the film found it necessary to make another film to be shown with *Death of a Salesman*. This was called *The Life of a Salesman* and purported to show that many salesmen were successful and happy, and that people like Willy Loman were untypical.

But for the overwhelming majority of audiences seeing this play political considerations have never been very important. For them, *Death of a Salesman* is the story of a particular family and it is from that point of view that we shall now consider it.

4.2 FAMILY RELATIONSHIPS

When the play was produced in China in 1983, the actors from the Chinese National Theatre were thoroughly aware of what political theatre can become. They were glad of an opportunity to work on a foreign play that was quite simply concerned with family relationships. Although they had some slight difficulties in understanding certain American conventions, the play was generally intelligible to them. In such matters as the relationship between a father and his sons or between husband and wife, or two brothers of differing natures or of the whole family with neighbours, they said that there were already plenty of examples of Chinese drama and they believed that there was very little basic difference between the Chinese and the Americans.

It is very likely that most people in the countries in which the play has been performed would agree with this statement, which would be supported by the history of drama from its beginnings. The ways in which the actions of the head of a family affect the lives of the other members have been reflected in countless plays in many languages from Greek tragedy onward.

Although it can be said that Willy lacks the nobility of stature to be the hero of a true tragedy, in his moment of triumph in death he acts very much as if he were. Even though it is brought about by a motor accident rather than by ritual poisoning or the sword of execution, there is an element of self-sacrifice in his death. Moreover, like most heroes in classic tragedy, he is motivated by a desire to see his family continue from generation to generation increasing in numbers and power. Willy really does seem to see his family as if it were a chosen dynasty. While his sons are still young, he tries to educate them in the best traditions of his own country, which he regards as the greatest in the world. However, he is aware that he has had very little contact with his own father, so he turns to his elder brother, Ben, for reassurance. Ben gives him a strange answer about the diamonds that can be found in the jungle. This poetic utterance resembles a soothsayer's riddle (Act I, Sequence 8). The saying is repeated in a different form at the end of the play. The diamonds are now to be found in the darkness (Act II, Sequence 12). All this suggests that this salesman from Brooklyn has dreams in which he sees himself, perhaps unconsciously, as a father figure in a Homeric myth.

When the young Biff seems to be promising greatness (or at least, greatness according to Willy's standards), everything is going well according to the scenario of Willy's dream of greatness for the family. When Biff fails maths and goes to Boston to ask his father for help, he discovers an unpleasant truth about Willy which destroys the relationship between them. Biff's faith in his father is destroyed, but Willy does not entirely give up hope. He thinks that Biff, drifting from job to job in the West, may be like a young hero who must pass through a period of trial in exile before returning to inherit his golden future (Act I, Sequence 1). Perhaps out of a sense of guilt, or perhaps out of a frantic desire to make the dream come true, Willy makes sacrifices for Biff. He sells the diamond watch-fob (a 'magic gift') that Ben gave him to pay for a correspondence course so that Biff may become an engineer (Act I, Sequence 9).

The strain of the secret knowledge that both men share and keep hidden from the rest of the family distorts the vision that they have of each other. To Biff, Willy has become 'a phony little fake', shameful to acknowledge as a parent. To Willy, Biff, the casual itinerant worker and self-confessed thief, is impossible to fit the cherished image of the handsome high school captain as he remembers him. 'Like a young god. Hercules and the sun, the sun all around him. Remember how he waved to me? Right up from the field, with the representatives of three colleges standing by? And the buyers I brought, and the cheers when he came out – Loman! Loman! Loman! . . . a star like that, a magnificent, can never really fade away!' (Act I, Sequence 9).

The key word here is 'magnificent'. Dictionary definitions of this word usually use terms such as 'splendour', 'great wealth' and associate the word with the idea of royalty. The poetic imagery of this speech suggests that to Willy the occasion he is describing is much more than a high school football match. To him it seems to have had the glamour of a ritual in which his son, the young prince, proves his nobility in the presence of the wise men from the three colleges and the buyers who are Willy's wealthy friends. To Biff, although it may have been a wonderful experience, it was a football match, no more and no less. It is Willy's tendency to dramatise his life, to raise it high above the ordinary that makes it impossible for him to accept that Biff is 'a dime a dozen' as he is himself. Willy can only explain Biff's behaviour as being motivated by spite and even when he realises that Biff does indeed still love him deeply he clings to his dream of magnificence. All the other relationships in the play are subservient to the central relationship between father and son with its pattern of early innocent love followed by betrayal by the father and a final reconciliation.

In order to understand the origins of Willy's dreams of grandeur for the Loman family it is necessary to go back into the history of the United States. Willy was born, the second of two sons, in the West in 1885. He was deserted by his father while he was still quite young. When he asks Ben for information in Act I, Sequence 9, he learns that he is descended from an extraordinary man with many talents and abilities. Loman senior was a pioneer, one of those who opened up the West in the face of many perils. He was an inventor, a musician, a maker of flutes and, incidentally, a salesman. Although he is never seen by the audience, whenever he is present in Willy's mind a change takes place in the atmosphere of the play. In such moments Willy tends to behave as if he were like his father, a legendary character, above and beyond ordinary everyday life. In production, this change of atmosphere is brought about by the use of the flute music. Willy is rightly proud of his heritage as the son of a pioneer, but this pride has led him into a tragic confusion of mind. Quite simply, he has come to believe that there are some men who possess virtue within themselves so that they can achieve success not by working hard for it but simply by being 'very well liked'.

The Lomans are not the only family mentioned in the play. Roughly parallel to the three generations of Lomans there are the three generations of Charley's family, including Bernard's two children, and three generations of Wagner's including Howard's two children. These two families are set in deliberate contrast to the Lomans. Charley (we never learn his surname) is a sensible and unpretentious man and a friend to Willy although Willy treats him badly. His son Bernard is a good student and works hard. Consequently he becomes a very successful attorney early in life. He has two children and so it seems that Charley's family life will continue and prosper.

Frank Wagner, Willy's old employer, and a good friend to him, had a son, Howard, who also has two children. His family line will also continue, although, unlike Charley's, it will remain at much the same level of prosperity. Willy Loman's father had two sons. Of these, the elder, Ben, made a great fortune and left seven sons to enjoy it and possibly build upon it. Willy himself has two sons. Neither of them is especially prosperous and after them, in spite of Happy's regular promises to marry and settle down, there is little sign that posterity will continue through either of them.

It seems almost as though the play is not concerned with the fortunes of one family alone but of making a comment about the notion of 'family' itself and the collective ideas which either keep families alive or destroy them.

4.3 DREAMS, SELF-DECEPTION AND DISHONESTY

It is, of course, too soon to claim that the play will ever become accepted as a world classic on a level with Shakespeare's plays or those of the Greek tragic poets, but it is worth considering what qualities it possesses that might qualify it to survive well into the future. What is there in this story of an American salesman to make him as interesting to future generations as Hamlet is to us?

Strangely enough, the fact that Willy is a saleman may well be less important to an understanding of the *themes* of the play than the personal characteristics which drive him to self-destruction. Perhaps Willy would never have become a salesman if he had been true to his own nature. In the Requiem, Linda says, 'He was so wonderful with his hands.' The audience are reminded that Willy inherited a manual skill from his father but refused to use it in his working life. For some reason he always regarded the skills of the builder as being inferior to those of the salesman. Biff makes the comment, 'He never knew who he was.' A similar remark was made of King Lear by one of his daughters, Regan: 'he hath ever but slenderly know himself' (Act I, Scene 1).

At no time in the play are the goods that Willy sells ever mentioned, except when he tells Linda how many gross he sold on one of his trips. In fact the product is of so little importance that the audience never know what it is or whether it is good or bad of its kind. When Miller was asked what it was that Willy was selling, he answered, 'Himself'. This is true in two ways. First, he ends up by selling his life for $20,000. Secondly, it is also true that all his life he was selling himself by trying to be so 'very well liked' that the buyers would take his product simply for his sake.

However, to be a salesman in the United States during the 1940s was an occupation as typical of its time and place as that of a priest would be in medieval Europe. Willy can therefore be seen as a representative American accepting the current American beliefs, especially that success is open equally to all citizens; yet he also remains a recognisable human character with certain weaknesses. It is a natural human tendency to dream of success for ourselves and for those we love, but we must beware of substituting the dream for the reality as Willy does. It is also natural for parents to see their offspring as showing extraordinary promise but it is necessary to pay more thought to their education than Willy does. In life, there is a constant temptation to exaggerate our successes and to deny or to minimise our failures, even at the expense of not telling the truth. Above all, we all desire to be, if not loved, at least well liked. The strength of this play is that it shows how trivial weaknesses can destroy a man as surely as the committing of any major crime.

At first sight, it may seem absurd to compare Willy Loman with Prince Hamlet. Hamlet is altogether a more noble character than this ignorant and dishonest small-time salesman. Hamlet meets his death fighting a duel and is finally overcome by poison treacherously administered. Willy dies in a contrived motor accident. It remains true, however, that Willy's failings lead him as inevitably to his death as do Hamlet's. It is also true that both characters can be accepted as being representative of their times.

Miller himself, in his Introduction to the *Collected Plays*, has said he believes that the main causes of the more important actions taken by any individual person always lie partly within the psychology of the person concerned and partly within the society in which that person lives. It follows logically, therefore, that Willy's suicide is partly caused by psychological failings, such as his inability to distinguish between dream and deceit, and partly by American society which overrated the dream of success.

5 TECHNIQUES

This section is concerned with the various techniques used by the playwright to tell the story and develop the themes, and is divided into subsections dealing with characterisation, language, staging (including the use of music and lighting), the general theatrical effect and a summary to indicate how the other components interact.

Although great plays are frequently studied as works of literature in terms of the beauty and power of the language, the richness and variety of the characterisation and the narrative devices used by the writer, we should never forget that a play is intended for performance before an audience and is not a complete work of art until this takes place.

5.1 CHARACTERISATION

The fourteen characters can be thought of as forming natural groups according to their function within the structure of the play.

The first group, the Loman family, are the *principal characters* and are drawn in great detail. Each is an individual and it is easy for a reader to imagine their appearance and the way they move and speak.

Main supporting characters, such as Charley and Bernard, are also clearly drawn but they are rather more *types* than individual and complex characters like the principal members of the family. Their actions are important to the development of the plot and theme, but less so than those of the principals. Ben is another main supporting character but different from Charley and Bernard. His character is clearly outlined, but he fulfils a different function within the play. The character of the Woman is very important to the plot but she is drawn less realistically than Charley or Bernard. Howard Wagner is presented as an immediately recognisable type, interesting because he is not the usual 'boss' character, but not so well developed as to distract attention from Willy in an important scene.

The *minor characters* are in the play to help the plot along and sometimes illuminate one of the themes. Jenny, Charley's secretary, makes a very brief appearance in Act II, Sequence 1 simply to give the audience information as to where Willy has got to in the course of his day in New York City. Stanley, the young waiter, is necessary to establish the restaurant scene and to help Happy reveal some of his own character. The two girls, especially Miss Forsythe, add a touch of colour and comedy just before a highly dramatic scene. Of these, only Miss Forsythe is relevant to the theme.

There are fourteen characters in the full stage company required for the play. The second waiter is usually dispensed with, although he is useful to clear away the furniture at the end of Sequence 9. The actual number of actors needed does not depend entirely upon the artistic needs of a performance. Most producers feel more comfortable when there are small parts which can be filled by actors capable of understudying the major roles.

Before we go into the details of each part it is necessary to consider what *kind* of characterisation will be required. This depends upon the *form* and style of the play. As we have seen, *Death of a Salesman* has a unique structure (see Section 2). The dialogue which the characters are called upon to speak is *realistic*, at least for most of the time. That is to say the speeches are intended to sound like ordinary conversation, apparently without any theatrically or special language.

There are some exceptions to this which will be discussed later, but for the most part this play is written so that it can be acted in a *realistic* style. This style, now generally accepted, was being introduced into America in the 1940s by the members of the Group Theatre (see Section 1). Miller knew these actors and directors very well, having met them in his days at the Federal Theatre.

Playwrights sometimes describe the characters in a preface to published editions of their works, but they also take care to plant clues in the actual dialogue to help the character towards the realisation of the part. It is sometimes necessary, though, for an actor to be careful. In some editions of the play, Willy has a line in which he says that he is rather fat and 'foolish to look at'. Another salesman has compared him to a walrus (Act I, Sequence 3). This might suggest that Miller thought that it was important for Willy to be fat and wearing a drooping moustache, but in fact the lines were written into the play because they suited the first actor to play the part, Lee J. Cobb. Although Cobb was very effective, his performance was very different from the second American to play the part. This was Paul Muni, a much smaller man, who played Willy as a timid person. The latest Willy Loman was Dustin Hoffman, who first appeared in this play in the role of Bernard. One critic comparing Cobb with Hoffman wrote that the difference in the two performances was the difference 'between a walrus and a shrimp'. Most of the successful characterisations of Willy have been by actors who could create a feeling of being 'little', psychologically as well as physically. This part, like all the great parts in the theatre, is open to more than one interpretation.

The principal characters

Willy, Linda, Biff and Happy make up the Brooklyn branch of the Loman family. We might expect there to be a family likeness somewhere, but which of the sons should more resemble the father? The answer to this question is important to a director choosing his actors so that they will 'look right'. As with many questions about characterisation the answer can be found only by close textual study – that is to say by looking for clues. Willy says that his boys are 'built like Adonises' (Act I, Sequence 3). Even when we allow for his habitual exaggeration, we realise that both Biff and Happy are likely to be well built and good looking, because both were at least competent athletes at school and Biff was football captain. Both seem to be immediately acceptable to the stylishly dressed young women in the restaurant (Act II, Sequence 5). This tells the director something but does not answer his question, so he must look for further clues in the text.

Happy is probably most like Willy in character because he never sees through Willy's pretences as Biff does. As a boy, Happy needed to take exercise to keep his weight down (Act I, Sequence 3). Does this imply that he is naturally plump and has the psychological characteristics generally supposed to go with plumpness? This sort of question seldom arises when a play is studied merely as a piece of literature but it is very important when the script is being brought to life in the theatre. In practice, questions like these are usually resolved by compromise but only after a lot of reference to the text of the play.

All the actors who play the principal 'Brooklyn' roles, including Charley and Bernard, have the problem of changing their apparent ages by as much as seventeen years. For Willy, the span is longer. In performance, there is no time for elaborate changes of make-up. The author makes some suggestions in the script, such as Linda's hair ribbon, but they are not always acceptable to the actors.

To *attract* our interest a character has to be unusual in some way, but to *hold* our interest he needs to have quite ordinary recognisable characteristics so that we can easily *identify* with him and share his emotions. Apart from the dreams and deceptions that eventually destroy him, *Willy Loman* is a very ordinary man. He is 63 when we first see him at the beginning of the play and is therefore in his mid-forties when we see him in his prime in Act I, Sequence 3. The intervening seventeen years must have been increasingly difficult for him. Sixty-three is not really very old, yet Willy Loman commits suicide at that age out of depression caused by mental exhaustion.

Willy, in his days of health and happiness, would have been an immediately recognisable figure. He is middle aged, typical of his class in that he is married with two children. He is by no means a rich man but has a job which brings in a regular income large enough for him to be able to afford to move out from a big city and to take a mortgage on a small detached house in rural surroundings. It has a garden in which he grows vegetables and flowers and is surrounded by a small forest of beautiful elm trees. The house is quite small, only just large enough for its inhabitants, but Willy has spent much time and skill on additions and improvements. The late 1920s are an idyllic time for Willy and Linda. In spite of his tendency to see the past in a slightly rosy glow, it can be accepted that his memories of this period in his life are basically true.

The Lomans have two good-looking boys. The elder seems already set for a promising career. There is not a great deal of money to spare but thanks to Linda's housekeeping skill, they manage to get by. Relationships within the family seem basically happy, although Willy is prone to bursts of temper and self-contradiction. Sometimes he exaggerates unnecessarily and, although Linda does not know it, some of his irritation arises from his feelings of guilt.

The audience never sees Willy dealing with a customer. All the evidence of his success comes from Willy himself but his sales figures do not suggest that he was ever as brilliant as he likes to suggest he was. In moments of depression he confesses to having to work ten hours a day. The only other witness is Howard Wagner (Act II, Sequence 2) and he denies Willy's claims. However, Willy enjoys being a salesman and would never have been happy doing any other job. He regards the salesman as a kind of aristocrat and much superior to people who work with their hands.

Willy is happiest showing off to his sons and educating them into his own lifestyle. Regarding himself as a good American and believing that the boys should know something about the history and geography of their native land, he tells them that 'Boston is the cradle of the Revolution' and mentions important commercial landmarks that he has seen such as the Waterbury Clock. (This was erected by the first firm in America to manufacture timepieces by mass production and to market them by an intensive sales campaign.) Although not widely read and impatient of scholarship (to him, Bernard is 'a worm'), he has his own store of wisdom which he is willing to pass on. He teaches the boys in some detail how to clean and polish the car so that it presents a shining image of efficient prosperity. He encourages them to keep fit and to excel at sports, and warns them against taking an interest in girls too early in life and further warns them not to make promises because 'girls believe everything you tell them'. He also passes on sensible proverbial advice such as 'Never leave a job till you're finished'. His sons are completely devoted to him and lonesome when he is away. They have learnt to expect generous presents from him when he returns from his travels, and probably believe that the punch ball was autographed personally for them by the heavyweight champion of the world because Willy asked him. All Willy actually says is 'It's got Gene Tunney's signature on it!'

The picture that emerges is of a very ordinary man, not very clever or well educated, but a good father and altogether a hard-working American citizen. It is this mass of detail that makes his character recognisable, credible and sympathetic so that his downfall becomes all the more pitiful.

This study of Willy at one stage in his life is not a complete character study as yet. There have been some indications of the later state of Willy's mind in the two preceding chapters. The full picture will be complete when we have looked at the other characters to find out how they see Willy and how their picture of him differs from his self-image.

No other character is as completely drawn as Willy. *Linda*, although she shares with Biff the position of being the next most important person in the play, is by no means as detailed a portrait. There are practical problems facing the actress who plays the part. The writer gives stage directions for managing the timeswitches but they do not go very far towards solving artistic difficulties. The writer considerately gives her several pages off-stage between her exit at the end of Act I, Sequence 1 and her reappearance in the middle of Act I, Sequence 3, but the stage direction 'Linda enters, as of old, a ribbon in her hair, carrying a basket of washing' is not really very helpful to the actress who has to switch Linda's age from about forty to nearly sixty.

The 'present-day' Linda would probably look rather older than her age, while in the happy past she might very well look young. Her final appearance in the Requiem should make it obvious that she has accepted her widowhood and, with it, old age. The timeswitches are much more difficult for the actress playing Linda than for any other of the cast. Some of these difficulties arise from the way in which the character is written. For instance, she seems to exist in isolation, never leaving the house until the Requiem and nearly always being seen in the shadow of Willy himself. On the occasions in which Willy is not present she seems almost to be a different person. It is not easy to visualise Linda but it may help an actress coming new to the part to know that Mildred Dunnock who created it was, in fact, quite slim in build and consequently had to 'pad up' at several successive auditions to achieve what is sometimes called a 'comfortable figure' before she was accepted for the part. Miller gives no physical description of Linda and his note at the beginning of the play is not very helpful.

Most often jovial, she has developed an iron repression of her exceptions to Willy's behaviour – she more than loves him, she admires him, as though his mercurial nature, his temper, his massive dreams and little cruelties, served her only as sharp reminders of the turbulent longings within him, longings which she shares but lacks the temperament to utter and follow to their end.

Some people might say this implies that Linda has no existence of her own apart from Willy and that this is one reason why she is difficult to visualise from the script, yet the author's note must be accepted as the starting point in any attempt to play the part in the theatre.

If the play is thought of as a modern Morality (see later in this section) then Linda can be thought of as being almost an *abstract* character, perhaps as a personification of love. Her love manifests itself in two ways. For her sons she feels a love which she maintains even when she is justifiably angry with them. Her love for Willy is different and much deeper and almost akin to worship.

From the very beginning Linda knows more about Willy's financial affairs than he thinks. She also knows that he has attempted suicide so she is not altogether surprised at Willy's unexpected return. Her reactions are always simple. She is ready to suggest simple solutions for complex problems. 'Maybe it was the steering . . . maybe its your glasses . . . why not take an aspirin?' This apparent simplicity is purely superficial and disguises her subtlety. Knowing what she knows she seizes her chance to persuade Willy to ask Howard for a job in New York. She is glad to have both her sons visiting and sleeping in their old bedroom and even enjoys the smell of their shaving lotion. The uneasy relationship between Willy and Biff always makes her very unhappy. Gently, she chides Willy for always provoking Biff into argument, but she never seems strong enough to force Willy to tell her the cause of the rift between them. Because she is quite aware of Willy's exaggerations she accepts without comment the way in which he makes a rapid downward adjustment in his sales figures, but she is never aware of his infidelity.

When Willy is taking his walk in Act I, Sequence 9, she takes the opportunity to tell the boys about the real state of affairs at home, and she is unsentimental and quite ruthless in her attack on them for their neglect of their father. In Act II, Sequence 9, she is equally angry with them for ditching Willy in New York and, in a superb gesture, she stops herself from picking up the flowers which they had brought as a peace offering. 'Pick up this stuff, I am not your maid anymore.' But Linda realises that the final family row will not pass over. When Biff announces that he is leaving home for good, she tries to remain calm, saying, 'I think that's the best way, dear.' This seems a rather downbeat way for a mother to bid farewell to her favourite son, but Linda usually expresses herself like that.

She is very unhappy when Willy refuses to perform a final important ceremony by shaking hands with Biff, and although delighted to find that Willy has discovered that Biff loves him she becomes intuitively afraid when Willy insists on staying alone in the garden after the boys have gone in.

LINDA   (*to Willy*) Come, dear.

BEN   (*with greater force*) One must go in to fetch a diamond out.

WILLY   (*to Linda, as he moves slowly along the edge of the kitchen, toward the door*) I just want to get settled down, Linda. Let me sit alone for a little.

LINDA   (*almost uttering her fear*) I want you upstairs.

WILLY   (*taking her in his arms*) In a few minutes, Linda. I couldn't sleep right now. Go on, you look awful tired. (*He kisses her.*)

BEN   Not like an appointment at all. A diamond is rough and hard to the touch.

WILLY   Go on now. I'll be right up.

LINDA   I think this is the only way, Willy.

WILLY   Sure, it's the best thing.

BEN   Best thing!

WILLY   The only way. Everthing is gonna be – go on, kid, get to bed. You look so tired.

LINDA   Come right up.

At this moment in Act II, Sequence 12, Linda could feel that she might have won. Biff has stated his intention of leaving home but she would be thinking that now Willy realises that Biff loves him and was not trying to spite him then all will be well. She cannot, of course, see Ben nor does she hear him, but she begins to realise that Willy is no longer under her protection. He is in the power of an influence which she hates and has opposed in the past. Reluctantly, she obeys him as she has always done and goes into the house. Immediately she appears in her bedroom and maybe she is watching him. Her speech in the Requiem is that of a simple woman who has believed almost everything that Willy told her. She cannot understand what has happened ('Where are the people he knew?'). She seems to be puzzled as to how it is that although all their debts are paid, there is nobody to live in the house. Above, all, she cannot understand why Willy took his life.

Biff is the only character who changes radically in the course of the action. We seem him first as the boy who readily accepts his father's standards and values. When he discovers that his father is far from perfect, he rejects not only Willy but Willy's beliefs. The younger Biff is in many ways a very ordinary high school boy, accepting the adulation of his classmates, enjoying the excitement of the football field, glorying in his growing skill and proud of his captaincy of the school team. He knows that he is good looking and is fully aware that girls are attracted by him. Yet all this is subsidiary to his worship of his father. In Act I, Sequence 3 he offers Willy the greatest tribute that he is able to offer.

> BIFF   (*taking Willy's hand*) This Saturday, Pop, this Saturday – just for you, I'm going to break through for a touchdown.
>
> HAPPY   You're supposed to pass.
>
> BIFF   I'm takin' one play for Pop. You watch me, Pop, and when I take off my helmet, that means I'm breakin' out. Then watch me crash through that line!
>
> WILLY   (*kisses Biff*) Oh', wait'll I tell this in Boston!

Willy's proudest memory of Biff is the moment, referred to more than once in the play, when Biff fulfils this promise, but no sooner has Willy responded than Bernard enters bringing with him the shadow of the dark future.

> BERNARD   Biff, where are you? You're supposed to study with me today.

This moment is more fateful for both Willy and Biff than it might appear. Up to this point Biff is just another adolescent, a likeable and promising youngster who might be expected to grow out of his present arrogance and selfishness if only his father had been sensible. Willy could have persuaded Biff to stay in training but also to keep up the study but instead he belittles Bernard in front of Biff. Just when he should have pointed out to Biff that it might be to his advantage to study, he chooses this moment to preach the doctrine of being well liked.

    Biff now begins to behave more arrogantly than ever. In spite of his father's anger, his mother's anxiety and Bernard's concern for him, Biff's behaviour continues to deteriorate (Act I, Sequence 5). Willy in his typical self-contradictory way threatens to punish him but also instructs him to steal timber from the building site. He is now physically mature, strong enough to fell a tree and brave enough to accept Uncle Ben's challenge to a fight. Yet he remains näive enough not to understand how it was that he failed maths. He believes that his father will help him out of the difficulty because he thinks Willy will be able to persuade Mr Birnbaum to change the marks. At this period in his life, Biff is very like his father. He cannot believe that Birnbaum failed him because he gave the wrong answers in the exam but thinks it was out of spite because Biff had made him look ridiculous in front of the class.

The visit to Boston completely explodes Biff's faith in his father but it gives him no wisdom in return. During his voluntary exile in the West Biff remains in a state of arrested development. He has begun to realise this when in Act I, Sequence 2 he tells Happy, 'I'm mixed up, very bad . . . I'm not married, . . . I'm like a boy'. In the same sequence, when Happy asks him why he has become bashful with women he evades giving a full answer, but it is possible that the shock he received as an adolescent when he found Willy with the Woman is still having an inhibiting effect.

He cares for his mother much more deeply than Happy does. When, in Act I, Sequence 2, he overhears Willy's strange mutterings for the first time, he is angry at Willy and sorry for Linda. Throughout the play, except for his lapse in Act II, Sequence 7, his first concern is always for Linda. He kneels symbolically at her feet to retrieve the flowers in Act II, Sequence 10 thus accepting his share of the blame for deserting Willy. At this point, Biff is becoming more adult and willing to come to terms with his father. When Linda tells him that Willy is planting seeds in the dark, he reacts with shock and pity and goes immediately to help. In demanding truth from others he does not spare himself. In Act II, Sequence 12 he admits to being a thief. 'I stole myself out of every job since high school. I never got anywhere because you blew me so full of hot air I could never stand taking orders from anybody!' After this speech Biff tells not only Willy but the entire Loman family to 'burn that phoney dream'. He then goes upstairs prepared to leave home for good on the following day. As he does so, he orders Linda to put Willy to bed. It is the son who has grown up and the father who has become the child.

In many plays there is sometimes one character who is in the midst of the action but always fails to understand what is really going on and so learns nothing. Such characters are useful for the audience to use as psychological reference points. *Happy* is one of these. When he is first seen in Act I, Sequence 2 he reveals himself, quite unconsciously, as being self-centred, self-indulgent and dishonest. He is cheerful, as befits his nickname, but he is also crudely sexist. Referring to his first sexual experience, when he cannot even remember the girl's name, he says, 'Yeah, that was my first time – I think. Boy, there was a pig!' He is a constant womaniser, although he knows that Linda would be very glad to see him married. In moments of crisis he usually promises his mother that he will get married very soon, but generally he continues going from pickup to pickup, making conquests merely to satisfy his vanity. If he can play a dirty trick on a friend or colleague he will do so. ('That girl Charlotte I was with tonight is engaged to be married in five weeks . . . to one of the executives.') If the colleague that he is betraying happens to be of higher status than Happy, then so much the better. He has inherited many of Willy's faults but also some of his father's advantages. He can be very charming and knows how to flatter people, especially women. In Act II, Sequence 5, his 'chatting up' of Miss Forsythe is a masterpiece of its kind complete with a casual lying reference to having trained at West Point, the famous military academy. It is also a very neat trick to pretend to be a champagne salesman in order to introduce yourself to an attractive woman by asking her to sample your product. It is significant that Miss Forsythe, who is by no means inexperienced in such matters, actually does comply with his request to fetch a friend of hers to join them at dinner. He certainly seems to have learnt from Willy that 'girls always believe what you tell them'. Except in this particular sequence. Happy never initiates the action in the play and what he has to say is usually an echo of what has just been said or is what he thinks his listener would like to hear. Like Willy he is an exaggerator. He likes to call himself 'Assistant Buyer' when he is in fact a junior assistant to the actual Assistant Buyer and seems likely to remain so because his mind is seldom on his work. Also, he is not above taking a bribe and will take time off sometimes without his boss's permission, but always takes care to cover himself (Act I, Sequence 10).

At the end of the play he remains Willy's son and the heir to Willy's dreams. In spite of all that has happened and everything that has been said, Happy still believes that Willy did not die in vain. In the Requiem he says that Willy 'had a good dream. It's the only dream you can have. To come out number-one man. He fought it out here and this is where I'm gonna win it for him.' At this point Biff 'gives a hopeless glance' at his brother. Happy has not only failed to learn from Willy's fatal dreams but does not seem to have understood them.

Everybody has met a person like *Charley*. He is the dry humorist who never smiles. His jokes are ironical and never to the taste of Willy who consequently usually misunderstands them. Willy and Charley are such totally different characters that, but for the fact that they are neighbours with sons going to the same school, they would probably have never become friends. Willy is a talker and a dreamer; Charley is silent and down to earth. Yet it is Willy who can put up a ceiling and Charley who cannot. On the other hand, Charley manages his money well because his accounts are kept honestly, whereas Willy's accounting is haphazard and but for Linda would be ruinous. Charley never expresses any particular hope for Bernard, but Bernard becomes highly successful. Willy expects great things of his sons but neither achieves very much.

The two men constantly argue and frequently quarrel. Willy regards himself as intellectually superior to Charley because he has heard about vitamins and gives him advice about eating.

CHARLEY   Couldn't sleep good. I had a heartburn.
WILLY   Well, you don't know how to eat.
CHARLEY   I eat with my mouth.
WILLY   No, you're ignorant. You gotta know about vitamins and things like that.

This exchange from Act I, Sequence 7 is typical of both men. Charley can never resist ribbing Willy and Willy usually falls into his trap and starts to shout at him.

CHARLEY   What is it with those vitamins?
WILLY   They build up your bones. Chemistry.
CHARLEY   Yeah, but there's no bones in a heartburn.
WILLY   What are you talkin' about? Do you know the first thing about it?
CHARLEY   Don't get insulted.
WILLY   Don't talk about something you don't know anything about.

This snatch of dialogue ends with Willy shouting at Charley and Charley remaining calm, yet it is worth asking why Charley ever takes the trouble to help Willy as he does throughout the play for more than seventeen years.

In Act II, Sequence 4, when he makes his last payment to Willy he also makes him a practical offer, commenting upon Willy's basic philosophy at the same time.

CHARLEY   The only thing you got in this world is what you can sell. And the funny thing is that you're a salesman, and you don't know that.
WILLY   I've always tried to think otherwise, I guess. I always felt that if a man was impressive, and well liked, that nothing –
CHARLEY   Why must everybody like you? Who liked J. P. Morgan? Was he impressive? In a Turkish bath he'd look like a butcher. But with his pockets on he was very well liked. Now listen, Willy, I know you don't like me, and nobody can say I'm in love with you, but I'll give you a job because – just for the hell of it, put it that way. Now what do you say?'

Willy's answer is evasive, but Charley knows that for all Willy's bluster he is jealous of him. Willy's strange manner of speaking in this sequence makes Charley suspect that he is contemplating suicide, especially his remark that after all the travelling that he has done he thinks that he will 'end up worth more dead than alive'. This prompts Charley to give Willy a warning – 'Willy, nobody's worth nothin' dead . . . Did you hear what I said?'

It is ironical that in spite of Willy's life-long efforts to become well known and well liked Charley is the only real friend that Willy has. He and Bernard are the only mourners other than the immediate family at the funeral. Charley's final speech in the Requiem, although often quoted out of the context of the play, seems somewhat out of character. He is not contradicting Biff, neither is he blaming him for saying that Willy had all the wrong dreams and never knew who he was. He is simply pointing out that a salesman, after all, makes very little practical contribution to his product – 'He don't put a bolt to a nut, he don't tell you the law or give you medicine.' From Charley's point of view the salesman is constantly at risk and has to dream in the sense that he must identify with the product he is trying to sell. It may be that Charley's low opinion of salesmen is one reason why he encourages his son to become a lawyer.

The bespectacled and studious *Bernard* begins as a *type*, the stock figure of fun to be found in much juvenile fiction. To Willy, he is 'anaemic' and 'a worm' (Act I, Sequence 3). From the point of view of Willy it is right and proper that such a worm should serve a young Adonis like Biff, even to the extent of breaking the law by giving him the answers to examination questions. In Act II Sequence 4, the adult Bernard tells Willy why he did so.

> Because I'd thought so well of Biff, even though he'd always taken advantage of me. I loved him, Willy, y'know? And he came back after that month and took his sneakers – remember those sneakers with 'University of Virginia' printed on them? He was so proud of those, wore them every day. And he took them down in the cellar, and burned them up in the furnace. We had a fist fight. It lasted at least half an hour. Just the two of us, punching each other down the cellar, and crying right through it.

Although it can be said that Bernard, like Charley, is more of a *type* than a fully developed character, this speech goes a long way towards explaining his motivation.

When he asks Willy why it was that Biff gave up trying to do anything with his life after he had been to Boston, Willy defensively flies into a rage. It is not until Charley tells him that he realises that the boy whom he despised has become a highly successful young lawyer on his way to plead a case before the Supreme Court. It is to

Willy's credit that, before he leaves Charley for the last time, he asks him to apologise to Bernard for him. No matter how wrong Willy can be, he seldom apologises.

Ben differs from all the other characters in the play in that he speaks a different kind of *language* and has a different *function* within the structure of the play. Considered simply as a character for an actor to play, he seems larger than life. He makes his first appearance more as a ghost than a memory during Willy's card game with Charley (Act I, Sequence 5). Miller describes him as 'a stolid man, in his sixties, with a moustache and an authoritative air. He is utterly certain of his destiny and there is an aura of far places about him.' He is always visiting, never staying, always on his way to somewhere else and always a powerful influence on Willy. If Willy had accepted Ben's advice earlier, he could have escaped from small-scale sales-manship into a larger commercial world, but under the influence of Dave Singleman and also under pressure from Linda who never trusts Ben, he always lets the chance go by.

Ben is a rich man when he dies leaving seven sons. Even after his death he retains his power over Willy's imagination. Willy calls him back from the dead to give advice on the $20,000 insurance deal. His advice is both practical and cynical. His experience has taught him that magnificence can only be achieved if you have money behind you. Willy in Act II, Sequence 12 cries out in his love for Biff, 'That boy – that boy is going to be magnificent!' Ben's comment is simply, 'Yes, outstanding, with twenty thousand behind him.' Ben can also be regarded as a *symbolic* character to be treated *expressionistically* in production (see later in this section).

The *Woman* remains nameless. She is kept deliberately incomplete and never developed as a character because if she became too interesting then the play might become distorted. She is not in any way a rival to Linda and therefore must not be thought of as the 'other woman' in the usual sense of the term. She simply reflects certain aspects of Willy's character that he is unable to share with Linda, such as the coarser side of his sense of humour. She is not married and lives with her sisters whom she thinks are likely to be scandalised by her goings on. In Act I, Sequence 4 she would seem to be a buyer's secretary or telephonist because she says, 'I'll put you right through to the buyers', but in Act II, Sequence 8 Willy says that she is a buyer herself. (This may well be one of Willy's half-truths.) She has a lively sense of fun and on the night when they are disturbed by Biff she may well have been drinking. In fun, she teasingly tells Willy the truth about himself, 'Gee, you are self-centred! Why so sad? You are the saddest, self-centredest soul I ever did see-saw.' However, she can become suddenly hard. When Willy has virtually thrown her out she demands the stockings that are due to her before she goes. Her laugh is heard at various moments during the play, always as an ironic comment upon the action. Some critics see this as suggesting the laughter of the Fates in high tragedy.

Howard Wagner is in his mid-thirties. He has time to play with his tape recorder during business hours because he is not intensely interested in the affairs of the firm that he inherited from his father. He is quite content so long as it keeps ticking over well enough to keep his family in comfort. He listens to the same radio programmes as all his friends and engages in the same sort of hobbies. He bullies his wife and adores his children. He is not unkind and would probably not have fired Willy on this particular occasion if Willy had not annoyed him.

The remaining characters present few problems. *Miss Forsythe* and her friend *Letta* are young, pretty and stylish with a natural ability to attract men. The image they present is in itself a further reference to the main theme of the play. In their appearance and behaviour they remind the audience of the 'starlets', the glamour girls who flocked to Hollywood or frequented places where rich and powerful men might be encountered. Their intention is to enjoy themselves and possibly obtain a little money and power for themselves. To gain this they are willing to be 'well liked' in a rather special way. Stanley and Jenny are very small parts. *Jenny* is scarcely a character at all. As we have seen, she helps the plot along by setting the scene for Act II, Sequence 4. *Stanley* has some chance to develop as a character when he is flattering Happy in Act II, Sequence 5 and again when he is being sympathetic with Willy in Act II, Sequence 9.

The off-stage characters

These are, of course, never seen by the audience but are mentioned so frequently that they come to have a life of their own. They certainly affect the narration of the story and the development of the theme.

Willy's father is first mentioned in the conversations between Willy and Ben in Act I, but his invisible presence has been planted at the beginning of the play by the sound of his flute. His desertion of the family when Willy was still a small child could explain why Willy 'feels temporary' about himself in Act I, Sequence 8. We are never told the circumstances in which Willy's father left his wife and children and it would be pointless to try to build any psychological motivation around it. It may be more useful to consider Willy's father as a symbol of that part of Willy's nature which is in tune with the spirit of the pioneers who opened up the American West. Willy seems to have inherited very little from his father. It is true that he is a salesman but he lacks his parent's inventiveness and sense of adventure. As for the practical skills, although Willy possesses them, he consistently underrates them.

Dave Singleman is another legendary character. Willy tells his story to Howard Wagner in Act II, Sequence 2. In spite of the detailed touches in the story, such as Dave's green velvet slippers, he never appears to be quite real, and perhaps Miller did not intend him to be so. Every profession has its legendary characters about whom stories accumulate and Dave Singleman is one of these. If his name has any significance it is from the concept of being 'single'. That is to say, Dave is to be though of as 'a man on his own' or 'a man who is unique'. It could be that Willy did actually know him and it was because of him that Willy remained a salesman in spite of opportunities to do something different. This is the usually accepted version. But it could be true that Willy used the story of Dave Singleman as a reason for turning down Ben's offer to work for him in Alaska. In any case, whether the story is meant to be taken as literally true or not does not affect either plot or theme.

Mr Birnbaum is a very real character as seen through Biff's boyish eyes in Act II, Sequence 7. Driven to explain why Mr Birnbaum will not graduate him, Biff tells Willy that Birnbaum hates him and explains why.

> BIFF   Yes, sir! See, the reason he hates me, Pop – one day he was late for class so I got up at the blackboard and imitated him. I crossed my eyes and talked with a lithp.
>
> WILLY   (*laughing*) You did? The kids like it?
>
> BIFF   They nearly died laughing!
>
> WILLY   Yeah? What'd you do?
>
> BIFF   The thquare root of thixthy twee is . . . (*Willy bursts out laughing. Biff joins him*) And in the middle of it he walked in!

This story, in Act II, Sequence 7 could well be a childish exaggeration but even if it were true then it is the more shame to Biff that he mocked the man. Mr Birnbaum seems to have been a conscientious and efficient teacher and it is not his fault that his subject is scheduled just before football practice.

More than that, he is an important part of a *chain* of *causation* in the plot. Had Willy brought Biff up to study properly and to respect men of learning, then Biff would have studied more seriously and would not have insulted Mr Birnbaum. As it happened he failed to pass the examination by only four points. If he had not annoyed Mr Birnbaum he could still have graduated. Had he graduated he would have had no need to go to Boston. Had he not gone to Boston then he would not have found Willy with the Woman and he would have kept his boyish illusions intact. And so on. (Chains of causation like this constantly occur throughout the play. Look out for more.)

Bill Oliver is another off-stage character whose actions affect the plot. Another chain of causation can be developed out of Biff's attempt to get Bill Oliver interested in his scheme. Had Bill Oliver recognised Biff and welcomed him into the office to discuss his ideas, there might have been at least a chance that Biff would have been on his way to financial success at last, but this would not have been very likely because the whole project rested on an untruth. As he waits for Bill Oliver, Biff gradually realises that he has been 'kidding himself' for years. The story that Bill Oliver put his arm round him and said that he could always come to him if he needed help (Act I, Sequence 2) is unlikely to be true because Biff was under suspicion of theft when he left Bill Oliver's employ. Therefore he could expect no recognition and no help from Bill Oliver. The whole project is doomed from the beginning. Bill Oliver is not as vividly drawn as the other off-stage characters but he does not need to be. It is sufficient for the audience to know that he is rich and powerful and possesses a luxurious office. He is constantly surrounded by people who want to do business with him and when he moves this retinue of followers moves with him. Biff now begins to realise that, for people like Bill Oliver, people like Biff Loman simply do not exist. At this moment, Biff knows that he is 'a dime a dozen'.

Note on the names of the characters

Sometimes the names a writer gives his characters are intended to serve as descriptive labels. Shakespeare often did this with comic characters such as Bully Bottom and with more serious ones such as Titania whose name has mythological overtones.

It is not certain whether Miller chose the name 'Loman' to suggest that Willy is a low man. This could refer to the figures carved on a Red Indian totem pole, where the man at the bottom carries all the others on his back, but it is more likely that 'low man' could refer to a small man or a little man, physically or spiritually. Linda describes him to his sons as a little man but she points out that a little man can be as exhausted as a great man. Certainly, Willy is a man of little learning, little honesty and little worth. Even his sins are little ones. He commits no murder, no theft on a grand scale and no far-reaching treachery. Although he destroys himself, he does it through little deceits and little betrayals. Even the use of the first name 'Willy' rather than the stronger 'Bill' or the more adult 'William' (used only by Ben), suggests that although he has become the head of a family, he has not yet grown up.

It could be significant that neither of the Loman boys seems to have a proper first name. Happy tells Miss Forsythe in Act II, Sequence 5 that he was named Harold. Biff's name sounds strong and aggressive but also rather too comic for such a character. Willy sometimes calls him 'Biffo' which is even less dignified. The only reason that can be suggested for these names is that they reflect Willy's own immaturity.

5.2 LANGUAGE

The dialogue is written almost entirely in colloquial English as it was spoken in and around New York in the 1940s. Americanisms are few and mostly immediately translatable by reference to the context in which they occur. For instance, a British reader has no trouble in translating 'flunking math' into 'failing maths'. There is only one example of a phrase that changes its meaning by crossing the Atlantic. In Act II, Sequence 9, Stanley gives Willy a message from the boys: 'They said they will see you home.' In Britain, this could signify that the boys intended to *accompany* Willy home. The British equivalent for their message would be, 'The boys said they will see you *at* home.' The only other difficulties that the non-American reader is likely to face may arise from unfamiliarity with the American education system and the terminology of the games played. Generally, the play has a reputation for translating well.

Language and character

Miller always approaches the writing of dialogue with great care and forethought. For *The Crucible*, he devised a reconstruction of seventeenth-century colonial English and used it to powerful effect. The *style* and *idiom* of the dialogue is always appropriate to the general style of his plays. He has claimed that the playwright is 'the poet in the theatre' but *Death of a Salesman* does not at first sight read like a poetic play. With the exception of Ben, most of the characters speak nothing but ordinary everyday speech. Most of Willy's utterances are ungrammatical and full of vulgarisms. Phrases such as 'these goddam arch-supports are killing me' can scarcely be regarded as poetic. Even in his moment of agony when he is saying goodbye to his wife for the last time, there is no nobility in his speech.

> LINDA   *(calling from her room)* Willy! Come up!
> WILLY   *(calling into the kitchen)* Yes! Yes. Coming! It's very smart, you realise that, don't you, sweetheart? Even Ben sees it. I gotta go, baby, 'Bye! Bye! (Act II, Sequence 12)

There is a certain wild imagery about one phrase that he uses twice – once in Act I, Sequence 6 and again in Act II, Sequence 5. 'The woods are burning!' This could have been derived from the slang of his trade, possibly a play on words from the expression 'to be fired' in the sense of losing one's job. Hence 'The woods are burning. I was fired today.' In the imagination of the speaker a personal disaster becomes something bigger and more terrifying, like the forest fires of the American West.

It is true that some of his characteristic remarks have become if not proverbial at least quotable. In Act II, Sequence 2, he tells Howard, 'You cannot eat the orange and throw the peel away – a man is not a piece of fruit.' This is not a very impressive remark when we read it in cold print. It even seems slightly comic, but coming from a good actor at the right moment in the play it is strangely moving, partly because Willy gives us the impression of being a man whose feelings are stronger than his vocabulary. Even more famous remarks such as, 'Be well liked and you will never want', although it is both simple and sincere still remains a long way from poetry. Willy's language most nearly approaches being *lyrical* when he is speaking simply and sincerely. One example of this is in Act I, Sequence 3 when he tells the boys that 'America is full of beautiful towns and fine upstanding people'. The speech, already quoted, at the end of Act I recalling Biff leading out his team for the Ebbets Field match, is typical of Willy at his best. A phrase like 'and the sun, the sun all around him', has a natural beauty even although Willy betrays a lack of scholarship in thinking that Hercules was a god.

Willy is believable as a character because he is complex and not always consistent. Although he is not faithful to Linda and has sometimes lied to her he is sincere in his love for her. When he has been fired, this all comes out in one of his speeches in Act II, Sequence 5.

> WILLY I was fired, and I'm looking for a little good news to tell your mother, because the woman has waited and the woman has suffered.

Here again, Willy is speaking truth in simple language that has a natural naïve poetry of its own.

As a salesman, Willy uses language *professionally*. That is to say, he uses words in order to persuade the customer to buy. Although it is never directly stated in the play, it would be reasonable to suppose that because selling has become difficult for him, Willy has fallen into using a 'hard sell' technique. He tries to bully the customer into giving him an order by not listening to any objections but *driving* straight on. In the following extract from Act II, Sequence 5, he is trying to force Biff to tell the story of his meeting with Bill Oliver in the way that Willy *hopes* it has taken place.

> WILLY (*Driving*) So tell me, he gave you a warm welcome?
> HAPPY Sure, Pop, sure!

BIFF   (*driven*) Well, it was kind of –

WILLY   I was wondering if he'd remember you. (*to Happy*) Imagine, man doesn't see him for ten, twelve years and gives him that kind of a welcome!

HAPPY   Damn right!

BIFF   (*trying to return to the offensive*) Pop, look –

WILLY   You know why he remembered you, don't you? Because you impressed him in those days.

BIFF   Let's talk quietly and get this down to the fact, huh?

WILLY   (*as though Biff had been interrupting*) Well, what happened? It's great news, Biff. Did he take you into his office or'd you talk in the waiting-room?

BIFF   Well, he came in, see and –

WILLY   (*with a big smile*) What'd he say? Betcha he threw his arm around you.

BIFF   Well, he kinda –

WILLY   He's a fine man. (*to Happy*) Very hard man to see, y'know.

HAPPY   (*agreeing*) Oh, I know.

WILLY   (*to Biff*) Is that where you had the drinks?

BIFF   Yeah, he gave me a couple of – no, no!

Such is the power of Willy's persuasion that Biff almost believes that Bill Oliver actually gave him a couple of drinks, Once it becomes clear that Willy can use this 'driving' technique as a desperate way of forcing a sale, then the whole of this sequence becomes much easier to understand.

In contrast to Willy, Linda usually speaks simply and gently and tells people whatever is at the front of her mind at the moment. This is not to say that she is a shallow person. She has depths that she does not always reveal, especially when talking to Willy at moments of crisis. In Act II, Sequence 12, she is under great stress. It seems to her that Willy and Biff have at least come to understand each other and may possibly become reconciled. At the same time she is aware of danger emanating from Ben, who is invisible to her. To express this conflict of powerful emotions she has one simple line – 'Now come to bed Willy.It's all settled now.' This calls for tremendous skill on the part of the actress. In Act I, Sequence 10, when Willy is absent and she does not have to be careful about what she says, her speeches take on a new freedom. This sequence will be analysed in Section 6.

The Loman brothers contrast in speech as in other matters, and this is very apparent in Act I, Sequence 2 which should be studied as an example of economical character drawing. Happy is the more simple and consistent character of the two; Biff is much more complex. When Happy is telling Biff about Willy's habit of talking to himself, Biff is interested but no more. When Happy mentions that Willy seems to be talking to Biff in his mumblings, Biff starts asking sharp questions and becomes defensive.

HAPPY   . . . And you know something? Most of the time he's talking to you.
BIFF   What's he say about me?
HAPPY   I can't make it out.
BIFF   What's he say about me?
HAPPY   I think the fact that you're not settled, that you're still kind of up in the air.
BIFF   There's one or two other things depressing him, Happy.
HAPPY   What do you mean?
BIFF   Never mind. Just don't lay it all to me.

This is typical of Biff's touchiness whenever his relationship with his father is under discussion, but immediately he admits to feeling uncertain about himself.

HAPPY   But I think if you just got started – I mean – is there any future for you out there?
BIFF   I tell ya, Hap, I don't know what the future is. I don't know – what I'm supposed to want.

Later in the same sequence Biff shows himself to be a man of sensitivity capable of responding in his own way to the beauty of nature.

BIFF   . . . This farm I work on, it's spring there now, see? And they've got about fifteen new colts. There's nothing more inspiring or – beautiful than the sight of a mare and a new colt. And it's cool there now, see? Texas is cool now, and it's spring.

Happy tends to talk more than Biff and at greater length. He enjoys talking and will talk to anybody who will listen, but especially to attractive women, for whom he has a special line of talk. His speech resembles his father's in its enthusiasms and exaggeration. Like his father, he will bend to agree with any pleasant sounding idea suggested to him but he will never think it out critically.

HAPPY   (grabbing Biff, shouts) Wait a minute! I got an idea. I got a feasible idea. Come here, Biff, let's talk this over now, let's talk some sense here. When I was down in Florida last time, I thought of a great idea to sell sporting goods. It just came back to me. You and I, Biff – we have a line, the Loman Line. We train a

WILLY   couple of weeks, and put on a couple of exhibitions, see?

That's an idea!

HAPPY   Wait! We form two basketball teams, see? Two water-polo teams. We play each other. It's a million dollars' worth of publicity. Two brothers, see? The Loman Brothers. Displays in the Royal Palms – all the hotels. And banners over the ring and the basketball court: 'Loman Brothers'. Baby, we could sell sporting goods!

Although the Loman brothers are very clearly drawn and made distinctive from each other as adults, they tend to be much more alike as boys.

As may be expected, *Ben's* speech is different from that of every other character. He speaks in a rather old-fashioned style, accentuated by his habit of addressing Willy as 'William'. He is more than just an older brother to Willy. He speaks rather more like a rich uncle. On his first appearance (Act I, Sequence 8) he strolls about inspecting the place. His first line '. . . so this is Brooklyn, eh?' suggests that having seen all the places between Africa and Alaska, he is not very impressed by Brooklyn. His most famous line in Act I, Sequence 9 sets his image firmly in Willy's mind and in the minds of the audience:

BEN   William, when I walked into the jungle, I was seventeen. When I walked out I was twenty-one. And, by God, I was rich!

The 'diamond' image is used to great effect in the final sequence (Act II, Sequence 12). Ben's lines are deliberately spaced out through Willy's farewell to Linda like a magical incantation as if he is deliberately leading Willy to self-destruction. Isolated, the lines seem rather theatrical –

'The jungle is dark but full of diamonds, Willy'
'One must go in to fetch a diamond out'
' . . . A diamond is rough and hard to the touch.'
'it's dark there but full of diamonds.'

In the context of the scene, they are part of the dramatic pattern which works on several levels to fuse the language style, combining the poetic with the realistic.

As a high school student, *Bernard* tends to be irritatingly logical when talking to adults, as when he says, in Act I, Sequence 3, 'Just because he printed University of Virginia on his sneakers doesn't mean they've got to graduate him, Uncle Willy!' The elder, and more successful, Bernard can afford to be more relaxed and casual in his speech (see Act II, Sequence 4).

Stanley has the glib style of a waiter who is also something of a salesman. He wishes to have Happy's continued custom, so he flatters him.

> STANLEY Sure, in front there you're in the middle of all kinds a noise. Whenever you got a party, Mr. Loman, you just tell me and I'll put you back here. Y'know, there's a lotta people they don't like it private, because when they go out they like to see a lotta action around them because they're sick and tired to stay in the house by theirself. But I know you, you ain't from Hackensack. You know what I mean?

This speech helps to add a few touches to the character of Happy and also makes Stanley into a more interesting character than just being 'a waiter', but it is a good example of the way in which language can be used to set the scene. In his speech, Stanley is describing the restaurant for the benefit of the audience. It is a city restaurant which attracts many people from the country, but also has private rooms for the benefit of New Yorkers in the know. It also prepares the way for a very important development – a highly dramatic confrontation between Willy and Biff. As it would not seem credible for two guests to be shouting at each other in a public place, Stanley is introduced to establish the idea of the private corner and so that Willy can have somebody to speak to about his memory of Boston when he returns from the washroom and finds that he has been deserted by the boys.

Miss Forsythe provides not only some pleasant comedy which contrasts with the high tension to come later in the sequence, but does so in a way which also maintains the main *theme* of the play.

> HAPPY Why don't you bring her – excuse me, miss, do you mind? I sell champagne, and I'd like you to try my brand. Bring her a champagne, Stanley.
> GIRL That's awfully nice of you.
> HAPPY Don't mention it. It's all company money. (*He laughs*)
> GIRL That's a charming product to be selling, isn't it?
> HAPPY Oh, gets to be like everything else. Selling is selling, y'know.
> GIRL I suppose.
> HAPPY You don't happen to sell, do you?
> GIRL No, I don't sell.
> HAPPY Would you object to a compliment from a stranger? You ought to be on a magazine cover.

GIRL   (*looking at him a little archly*) I have been. (*Stanley comes in with a glass of champagne.*)

HAPPY   What'd I say before Stanley? You see? She's a cover girl.

STANLEY   Oh, I could see, I could see.

HAPPY   (*to the girl*) What magazine?

GIRL   Oh, a lot of them. (*She takes the drink*) Thank you.

If Miss Forsythe really is a cover girl as she claims then she would have been one of those pin-up pictures which were treasured by thousands of young men. To them she would have been the beautiful but unattainable dream-girl. But she does not say which magazine carries her picture. Is she, like Willy Loman, a self-deceiver? Or is she a deliberate deceiver?

This piece of dialogue keeps the play moving along in an entertaining way but also reminds the audience of the *theme* of dreams, self-deception and deceit. (Happy, by the way, is lying with intent to deceive in his first speech in the passage quoted above.)

5.3   STRUCTURE AND NARRATIVE TECHNIQUES

However we may classify the play, we must admire its distinctive *structure*. It will be seen from the simplified Chart of Sequences (pages 66–7) that the story is told on two different levels. As has been shown earlier, there is the 'public' storyline which begins late one night and ends twenty-four hours later. Parallel with this, there is the 'private' storyline inside Willy's mind, which like our own minds, does not always work logically and chronologically but mixes up memories and imaginings with what is actually taking place in the present. Although this may appear to be rather complicated when set out on paper, it works in the theatre, even though the play has been produced in countries with markedly different theatrical traditions.

Indeed, audiences in countries where the theatrical conventions are mainly *non-realistic* have had no difficulty in understanding the play. Even in Western theatre, *expressionism* has been an accepted convention for about fifty years, partly because of the influence of the cinema. The term *expressionism* is also used in the visual arts, but in theatre and cinema it is usually defined as being a mode of writing and production in which the aim is to depict *inner meaning* rather than *outward appearance*. For writers, this may imply the use of poetic or stylised language and symbolic characterisation. For producers, it implies the use of non-realistic scenery and effects. The movement towards expressionism began in Germany, and was used in America by writers such as Elmer Rice, who was the first stage writer to use the cinematic *flashback* technique in a play called *On Trial* (1914). Other playwrights, such as Eugene O'Neil, have written plays like *Emperor Jones* (1922), in which the action takes place partly in the actual present and partly in the memory of the central character. The British playwright, J. B. Priestly, has experimented with time-changes in more than one play, notably in *I Have Been Here Before* (1937).

In expressionist plays the following effects are likely to be used. Many of them occur in *Death of a Salesman*.

1. The supposed time may be past, present or future and the action may flow without interruption from one time period to another. More than one time period may coexist, that is to say the audience may see present and past action at the same time.
2. The action may be presented as a dream or a vision by one of the characters.
3. The action may take place in more than one location simultaneously.
4. Music and light may be used to indicate a character's state of mind.
5. Settings may be non-realistic or partly realistic. That is to say, one part of the stage may be set with realistic scenery, such as the kitchen at Brooklyn, but this may have an empty open stage area in front of it into which a single piece of furniture or other item may be brought to suggest a location, or the area may be left empty and used for a variety of purposes, such as the garden at Brooklyn.
6. Some characters may be totally non-realistic, abstract or even non-human. This does not apply to *Death of a Salesman*, although it could be argued that Ben is not entirely a realistic character.

It might be expected that the 'public' action sequences would be written realistically and the 'private' action sequences would be expressionist. Before making up your mind about this, look through the play making reference to the Chart of Sequences. You may well discover that there is no fixed rule, partly because the writer uses the *timeswitch* differently at every change of sequence.

Miller did not use either the timeswitch or the mixture of realist and expressionist narration techniques simply for their own sakes but because he found that this was the best way to tell the story with the minimum of delay and repetition. Each sequence contains as much information as is necessary but does not last any longer than it need. Pick any sequence you choose and test this statement by trying to cut lines or stage directions.

We have seen that the main plot of the play is very simple, but it contains a number of *sub-plots*, each with its own *chain of causation*, in which one action leads to another though sometimes after the passage of time. One such chain begins in Act I, Sequence 2, when Biff first has the idea of approaching Bill Oliver and ends in Act II, Sequence 7 when he realises that he can never again approach him with a business proposition. Even so, his failure to make a deal has an effect on the main plot in his argument with Willy in Act II, Sequence 12. There is another chain which could be called the 'job in New York' chain, beginning in Act I, Sequence 1 and joining the main plot towards the end of Act II. All these chains of causation interconnect with each other and with the main plot. Use the Chart of Sequences to compile a diagram of the connections.

Besides telling the story, the playwright must keep his audience interested by changing the *mood* fairly frequently. For instance, Act II begins in a mood of expectancy and optimism, but the phone call from Biff to Linda slightly dampens her pleasure when she is reminded of the rubber tube that Willy might have used to commit suicide. Howard's entry changes the mood again. The audience are interested in Howard because he is a new character of whom they have heard. They are amused by the various voices coming out of the recorder, but the tension builds with Willy's growing impatience as he tries to gain Howard's attention. It is possible to compile a sequence chart showing how the mood changes throughout the play.

CHART OF SEQUENCES

'PUBLIC' ACTION IN PRESENT TIME
(more or less continuous over twenty-four hours in chronological order)
The audience sees *objectively* from outside Willy's mind.

'PRIVATE' ACTION OR REMEMBERED ACTION
(ranging backwards in time, but not chronologically)
The audience sees 'from inside Willy's mind'.

Act I

Sequence
1. Willy comes back to Brooklyn
2. Biff and Happy discuss their lives

Sequence

3. Willy remembers the past in Brooklyn
4. He is reminded of the Woman in Boston
5. He returns to Brooklyn in the past

6. Willy and Happy are joined
   by Charley
7.   Private and public worlds overlap
   Charley and Willy play cards   Ben appears to Willy
                          8. Ben visits Brooklyn
9. Willy takes a walk. Linda tells
   the boys how bad things
   are. Biff tells Willy about his
   idea of approaching Bill
   Oliver

Act II

Sequence	*Sequence*
1. Brooklyn next morning. Willy goes off to New York.	
2. Howard's office. Willy is fired	
	3. Ben visits Brooklyn. Willy and the boys go to the Ebbets Field game
4. Charley's office. Willy meets the adult Bernard and borrows his insurance premium from Charley	
5. New York restaurant. Happy dates Miss Forsythe. Willy and Biff begin to argue	

             Private and public worlds begin to overlap
                    6. Bernard tells Linda that Biff
                       has 'flunked math'

7. Willy continues disagreement with Biff
             Private and public worlds overlap with
             switching from present to past and back
                     8. Boston hotel bedroom. Biff
                        discovers Willy's affair with
                        the Woman
9. Restaurant: Stanley helps
   Willy
10. Boys return home. Willy
    plants seeds
11.   Public and private worlds overlap
    Final confrontation between   Willy and Ben discuss the
    Willy and Biff $20,000 death deal
12. Willy goes to his death

5.4   THE PLAY IN THE THEATRE

For all its complex originality, *Death of a Salesman* would not work in
the theatre had the playwright not paid attention to such apparently
trivial matters as, for example, the arrangement and timing of
entrances and exits for the actors. Draw up a timetable for every
principal actor to indicate the sequences in which he is on or off the
stage. Consider also whether the actor has to 'move in time'
backwards or forwards for his next entrance. What costume changes
might this involve? Does the playwright give instructions for costume
changes in sufficient detail? Is it enough for Linda simply to put a
ribbon in her hair to indicate that she is seventeen years younger? In
this context, some other interesting questions arise, namely, does the
actor playing Ben need to age physically over the total time of his
appearances? If not, why should this be so?

Once you have compiled these timetables you will discover that no
actor is under too much stress. Even the actor playing the part of
Willy has moments of rest. It takes more skill from the writer than is
generally realised to arrange such matters. (It is worth noting that
Shakespeare frequently arranged his plot in order to give his leading
actor a period of rest off-stage just before the climax of the play.)
These off-stage times are not merely for rest, of course, nor simply
for technical changes but also for the more important psychological
changes required by the actors.

Miller is unusually specific in his stage directions. Very often, a
playwright will present a play to the director without having thought
about practical matters at all and will be content to leave set design,
lighting and music to other people. *Death of a Salesman* is unique in
that it can be effectively performed only on the set as specified by the
writer and as originally designed by Jo Mielzener. Lighting and music
should also aim to meet Miller's specification. The whole *stage-
management* side of the performance arises directly from the written
script to form a complete artistic unit.

Mielzener's design has been modified slightly in the productions
since 1948. Generally, most directors have dispensed with the
transparent curtain with the green vegetation which was originally
lowered over the house for the 'remembered' sequences. (See the
stage direction leading into the first timeswitch to Act I, Sequence 3.)

The set works very well, especially when the action is in Brooklyn,
if the lighting and music cues are correctly followed. The exit of Biff
and Happy from their bedroom at the end of Act I, Sequence 2 may
be rather difficult for the actors because they have to do it unseen by
the audience, perhaps in the dark or a dim light and down a ladder,
but most of the other changes present very few difficulties. Some of
the settings in Act II, such as the scenes in the offices and the
restaurant appear to be rather obviously contrived. In the theatre,

the use of lighting and sound together with the natural dramatic strength of the action maintains the tension. The lighting throughout fulfils two functions. First of all, it indicates time of day and season of year in a more or less realistic way, but it also indicates *mood*, especially Willy's changing moods. There should also be something in the use of lighting to support the other changes that take place during the timeswitches. For instance, the match at Ebbets Field would have taken place towards the end of the American football season. Football is played in all sorts of weather in real life, but Willy remembers this match as an occasion of triumph, so it is not an accident that Biff's team plays in a gold uniform and Willy remembers 'the sun all around him'.

Go through the play looking for *light cues* and try to work out which part of the stage would be lit and in what colour. Pay attention both to the requirements of realism and the evocation of mood. The sound plot is written into the published editions, but it is not very specific. It would be an interesting challenge to a composer who had never seen the play to write the tune for the flute which Miller describes as being 'small and fine, telling of grass and trees and the horizon'. If you have musical talent it might be worth trying, but it is more important to ask why Miller asked for such music and specified that it should be played on that particular instrument. It is probably connected with Willy's memories of his father, but it also evokes other emotions, generally nostalgic but difficult to define. It is likely that every member of the audience will react differently. There is other music in the play such as that which accompanies the appearances of the Woman. Perhaps this should be, like the lady herself, cheerful but rather loud. If you were directing the play, what kind of music would you ask for?

The first production of the play was costumed in its own period for the 'present day' sequences and the intention was to use the fashions of the past for the 'remembered' sequences. In fact, for the sake of convenience very little actual costume change was made. If you were directing the play today would you update the costume styles for the present-day sequences or would you recreate the fashions of the 1940s? Your decision would depend upon what you considered to be the main *theme* of the play. If the production was intended to call attention to conditions in America in the 1940s through presenting the story of the life and death of a hardworking and exploited travelling salesman, then obviously the clothing, furniture and details of the set should be true to the period. If the intention is to consider the effect upon a family of a father who tries to live for a dream and never tells the truth to himself or to other people, then presumably setting, lighting, music and costume can become more symbolic and expressionist and less realistic so that the period setting of the play become irrelevant.

Although decor is very important, the life of the play in the theatre depends on the actors. Some of the acting that took place in the theatres of Britain and America in the 1940s would appear rather melodramatic and 'over the top' to modern audiences. Actors were frequently typecast and their technique was dominated by cliché, with certain gestures and facial expressions in regular use to *indicate* rather than to *express* emotion. Plays were often stereotyped and frequently written to suit the mannerisms of popular performers. *Death of a Salesman* was a very unusual play for the period in which it was first produced and called for an equally unusual company of actors. Miller was one of a group of writers, actors and directors who had been associated with the New York Group Theatre. This was dedicated to exploring new theatrical techniques in order to express new social ideas, and included such writers as Clifford Odets, author of *Waiting for Lefty* (1935), Maxwell Anderson who wrote *Both Your Houses* (1933), which won the Pulitzer prize, and Tennessee Williams, who was to become world famous with *A Streetcar Named Desire* (1949). The directors included Lee Strasberg and Elia Kazan, the latter being the first director of *Death of a Salesman* with Lee J. Cobb as Willy Loman.

6 SPECIMEN PASSAGE AND COMMENTARY

The following example shows how to analyse a selected passage from the play. The extract is from Act I, Sequence 9. In some ways it is untypical of the play because the action takes place on one of the few occasions when Willy is off-stage. This fact in itself makes it interesting. Read the passage through carefully, making your own notes as you go *before* you refer to the Commentary.

LINDA   You're such a boy! You think you can go away for a year and . . . You've got to get it into you head now that one day you'll knock on this door and there'be strange people here –

BIFF   What are you talking about? You're not even sixty, Mom.

LINDA   But what about your father?

BIFF   (*lamely*) Well, I meant him too.

HAPPY   He admires Pop.

LINDA   Biff, dear, if you don't have any feeling for him, then you can't have any feeling for me.

BIFF   Sure I can, Mom.

LINDA   No. You can't just come to see me, because I love him. (*With a threat, but only a threat, of tears*) He's the dearest man in the world to me, and I won't have anyone making him feel unwanted and low and blue. You've got to make up your mind now, darling, there's no leeway any more. Either he's your father and you pay him that respect, or else you're not to come here. I know he's not easy to get along with – nobody knows that better than me – but . . .

WILLY   (*from the left, with a laugh*) Hey, hey, Biffo!

BIFF   (*starting to go out after Willy*) What the hell is the matter with him? (*Happy stops him*)

LINDA   Don't – don't go near him!

BIFF   Stop making excuses for him! He always, always wiped the floor with you. Never had an ounce of respect for you.

HAPPY   He's always had respect for –

BIFF   What the hell do you know about it?

HAPPY   (*surlily*) Just don't call him crazy!

BIFF   He's got no character – Charley wouldn't do this. Not in his own house – spewing out that vomit from his mind.

HAPPY   Charley never had to cope with what he's got to.

BIFF   People are worse off than Willy Loman. Believe me, I've seen them!

LINDA   Then make Charley your father, Biff. You can't do that, can you? I don't say he's a great man. Willy Loman never made a lot of money. His name was never in the paper. He's not the finest character that ever lived. But he's a human being, and a terrible thing is happening to him. So attention must be paid. He's not to be allowed to fall into his grave like an old dog. Attention, attention must be finally paid to such a person. You called him crazy –

BIFF   I didn't mean –

LINDA   No, a lot of people think he's lost his – balance. But you don't have to be very smart to know what his trouble is. The man is exhausted.

HAPPY   Sure!

LINDA   A small man can be just as exhausted as a great man. He works for a company thirty-six years this March, opens up unheard-of territories to their trademark, and now in his old age they take his salary away.

HAPPY   (*indignantly*) I didn't know that, Mom.

LINDA   You never asked, my dear! Now that you get your spending money someplace else you don't trouble your mind with him.

HAPPY   But I gave you money last –

LINDA   Christmas-time, fifty dollars! To fix the hot water it cost ninety-seven fifty! For five weeks he's been on straight commission, like a beginner, an unknown!

BIFF   Those ungrateful bastards!

LINDA   Are they worse than his sons? When he brought them business, when he was young, they were glad to see him. But now his old friends, the old buyers that loved him so and always found some order to hand him a pinch – they're all dead, retired. He used to be able to make six, seven calls a day in Boston. Now he takes his valises out of the car and puts them back and takes them out again and he's exhausted. Instead of walking he talks now. He drives seven hundred miles, and when he gets there no one knows him any more, no one welcomes him. And what goes through a man's mind, driving seven hundred miles home without having earned a cent? Why shouldn't he talk to himself? Why? When he has to go to Charley and borrow fifty dollars a week and pretend to me that it's his pay? How long can that go on. How long? You see what I'm sitting here and waiting for? And you tell me he has no character? The man who never worked a day but for your benefit? When does he get the medal for that? Is this his reward – to turn around at the age of sixty-three and find his sons, who he loved better than his life, one a philandering bum –

HAPPY   Mom!

LINDA   That's all you are, my baby! (*to Biff*) And you! What happened to the love you had for him? You were such pals! How you used to talk to him on the phone every night! How lonely he was till he could come home to you!

BIFF   All right Mom. I'll live here in my room and I'll get a job. I'll keep away from him, that's all.

LINDA   No, Biff. You can't stay here and fight all the time.

BIFF   He threw me out of this house, remember that.

LINDA   Why did he do that? I never knew why.

BIFF   Because I know he's a fake and he doesn't like anybody around who knows!

LINDA   Why a fake? In what way? What do you mean?

BIFF   Just don't lay it all at my feet. It's between me and him – that's all I have to say. I'll chip in from now on. He'll settle for half my pay cheque. He'll be all right. I'm going to bed. (*He starts for the stairs*)

LINDA   He won't be all right.

BIFF   (*turning on the stairs, furiously*) I hate this city and I'll stay here. Now what do you want?

LINDA   He's dying, Biff.

Commentary

Examiners frequently set such a passage for commentary. It is a good idea to read the passage *more than once* making notes as you go. Then begin to gather your ideas under different headings.

1 Context

Whereabouts in the play does the extract occur?
In this case, it occurs towards the end of Act I, while Willy is taking his walk and Linda is left alone with the boys.

What has happened before this extract begins?
Keep your comments *brief* here. It is enough to say that Willy's behaviour since he returned home has been causing Linda even more anxiety than before. Because Biff has been away working in Texas for a year and Happy, although living in New York, seldom visits Brooklyn, she has had no chance to speak to them frankly.

2 Location

This should be noted with reference both to *time* and to *place*, and is particularly important because of the unique structure of this play. The place is the kitchen in the house at Brooklyn and the time is the present, at night. The action is public, that is to say it does not take place inside Willy's mind.

3 Plot and action

What happens during the extract?
There is certainly very little physical action during the scene, but a great deal of psychological tension between Linda and the boys, especially between Linda and Biff. It is revealed in the manner in which *language* is used by the characters.

4 Character

How far does the extract reveal or develop the characterisation?
The main character in this extract is Linda who, up to this point in the play, has appeared as a rather conventional and almost stereotyped figure. In her earlier scenes the audience have seen her coping patiently and gently in the present with all the troubles that Willy is giving her. In the past she has appeared as a loving mother to her sons but not offering her love for them in competition with his. She is loyal and admiring to Willy but also keeps her eye firmly on the family finances. This scene reveals further details and greater depths in her character.

Biff's first speech tells the audience that Linda is younger than Willy ('. . . not even sixty yet'). Her reply shows that she is already aware that death may be near. ('One day you'll knock on this door and there'll be strange people here . . . ') Linda is not the sort of woman who will habitually use her tears in emotional blackmail but there is a stage direction (. . . *a threat, but only a threat, of tears*) which indicates how strongly she feels about forbidding one of her sons to visit the house if he cannot agree with her husband. She loves them both. She is aware that Willy is 'not easy to get along with' and she admits that she, more than anyone else, knows about the worst side of his character. Nevertheless, she demands that Biff shows respect to Willy and prevents Biff from going to speak to him when he is heard muttering strangely outside. She also has her secret fears about Willy's mental stability, but when Biff says that Charley is in many ways better than Willy, she flares up to defend her husband in a series of very strong speeches, not only outlining the whole process of Willy's decline but demanding that Biff and Happy do their duty as sons and 'pay attention' to the needs of their father.

There is no doubt that her love for Willy is far stronger than her love for her sons. She does not hate them, although they have given her cause. In fact even while she is firmly and bluntly telling them the truth about themselves she uses habitual little endearments. She calls Happy 'a philandering bum', but she adds, almost tenderly, 'that's all you are, my baby!' This reminds us that Happy is her last-born child who she may have cossetted a little and whom she regards as being rather immature.

To Biff, although she says 'you're such a boy!', she speaks with more respect and with greater sorrow: ' . . . And you! What happened to the love you had for him? You were such pals! How you used to talk to him on the phone every night! How lonely he was till he could come home to you!'

She presses Biff to tell her why he always says that Willy is a fake. To Linda, Willy is not and never could be a fake. If he were proved to be so then her whole world would collapse. It is possible that she may have a secret fear that Biff may be right after all. (There is no direct evidence of this in the play, but it is an example of the sort of question that actors might discuss when trying to understand the characters.) Biff's character develops very little in this scene, which is predominately Linda's, but the audience learn that in spite of his bitter feelings towards Willy, he is willing to contribute half his pay to support his parents. This is obviously out of his love for Linda. He is also willing to stay and work in the city which he hates.

Happy has fewer speeches, partly because he is out of his depth and partly because he remains generally self-centred. He has never taken the trouble to ask Linda whether she needs any extra money and when he did give her some at Christmas it was quite inadequate. On the other hand, he resents Biff calling Willy crazy. By the end of the extract he has fallen into silence because he cannot understand the depth of emotion that is affecting both Linda and Biff.

5   Mood

Within the extract, the mood changes frequently, but the emotional tension is usually high. There is strong interaction between the three on-stage characters. Linda's mood is the most complex. Having decided that Happy is not likely to be of much help to her in the present crisis, she has turned to Biff. In a short scene immediately preceding this extract she has been asking him about his relationship with his father and his vagrant way of life. She is anxious for him to settle down at home, but he has given her no satisfactory answers and has tried to set a mood of tender playfulness with her to cover his evasiveness.

With great resolution, on the verge of tears, she presents Biff with an ultimatum forbidding him to come home to her unless he can also show affection towards Willy. This is impossible for Biff to accept and there is a momentary deadlock until the tension is broken by Willy's voice from outside, where he is heard chuckling and speaking playfully to the young Biff in a timeswitch. This very brief interlude of near-comic irony is immediately ended by the angry exchange which breaks out between Biff and Happy. Linda then takes control again. Speaking quietly and reasonably but with very deep feeling she defends Willy while admitting his failings. She suggests that he is not mad but merely exhausted. With one cause for anxiety removed the tension relaxes very slightly as far as the boys are concerned, but rises again immediately when Linda goes on to tell them that Willy is no longer getting a salary.

Happy's indignant denial of any knowledge of this causes Linda to turn on him and in her anger she releases all the emotions pent up during her months of loneliness. She is very angry with Willy's employers, and although deeply understanding and sympathetic towards Willy, she is bitterly disappointed with her sons.

Very briefly, the mood lightens partially when she writes off Happy as 'a philandering bum' but darkens again when she turns to Biff. She cannot understand why he despises his father. Then the mood softens as Biff partly relents and agrees to stay at home and contribute to the family income. The scene appears to be ending quietly as he moves to go upstairs but Linda stops him. He answers her roughly and it now seems as if another argument is about to break out, but Linda changes the mood again by telling Biff and Happy that their father is dying. The extract ends on a shocked pause, with the family united.

6   Language

Although the language seems to be realistic there are some deliberate poetic effects in Linda's longer speeches. For the most part, Biff and Happy speak in their usual short colloquial utterances such as, 'What the hell do you know about it?' and 'Charley never had to cope with what he's got to.' Biff has one dramatic phrase, 'Charley wouldn't do this. Not in his own house – spewing out that vomit from his mind.' But this is Linda's scene and her language not only reveals her character but has its own poetic strength.

Although the speeches are highly emotional, there is no sentimentality. If you examine the two long speeches you will discover that the words are very ordinary. Many of them are monosyllables. Yet these speeches are both poetic and moving. In the first speech there are a number of very short words in the sentence – 'he's not to be allowed to fall into his grave like an old dog'. The picture it evokes is simple but very sad. In the next sentence there is the repetition of the word 'attention'. The rhythm of the word and the repetition sound like a drum beat – 'attention, attention must be paid . . . ' Linda goes on to say how she imagines Willy suffers during his unsuccessful business trips. Once again the language is simple but vivid – 'He used to be able to make six, seven calls a day in Boston. Now he takes his valises out of the car and puts them back and takes them out again and he's exhausted. Instead of walking, he talks now. He drives seven hundred miles, and when he gets there no one knows him any more, no one welcomes him.' Following this, she asks the boys ten consecutive questions, with mounting merciless intensity until they begin to feel like criminals under cross examination from a prosecuting attorney.

7 Theme

The extract picks up one of the major themes in the play. It is a comment upon Willy from the viewpoint of two people who truly love him but see him differently. To Linda, who has always believed everything he has told her, Willy is a hero defeated by a cruel fate and needing attention, pity and love. To Biff, he is a fake, a liar and a cheat, getting what he deserves. Above all, Biff is angry that his mother, whom he also loves, is being made to suffer for his father's failings.

7 IN REHEARSAL

You will find it very illuminating to take any short scene from the play and treat it as if you were the director preparing to rehearse your actors for a performance. Better still it will be helpful to form a group, taking it in turns to direct each other and discussing the different ways of playing the scene, *always* with careful reference to the text of the play.

It is best to begin by considering the physical circumstances. You do not need a stage or scenery, neither need you memorise the parts. It will be sufficient to have a few chairs or tables and something to represent the steps. Now be prepared to find practical answers to a number of questions. In which area of the stage does the action take place? How are the actors positioned in relation to the set and to each other at the beginning of this scene?

If you look back to the previous scene, you will find that Linda went into the kitchen at the same time as Willy walked off the stage and Biff came downstairs. Happy joins them later and sits on the steps. In the course of the action, Linda, who is always busy, is sitting at the table mending Willy's jacket. This in itself is a significant action and true to her character. These positions are not likely to be held throughout the action of the extract. Happy will probably remain where he is because the main confrontation is between Linda and Biff. For most of the time, he is not involved. It is frequently true of Happy that he is more likely to be on the edge of the action than in the centre. However, in this scene there is a stage direction which indicates that Happy stops Biff from going after Willy when he is heard talking and laughing outside. This action goes with Happy's line, 'Just don't call him crazy!'

In order to direct the actors properly, the director has to *realise* the scene in his mind, so you should draw a plan of the set and *plot the moves* for each actor as you go along. At the beginning of the extract, where is Linda sitting and where is Biff in relation to her? There is a clue in his previous speech, and another in a stage direction a little before that. Since Biff must have touched Linda's hair he must have been standing close to her, possibly with his arm round her shoulders, showing affection. When Linda begins to speak, she moves away from him. Exactly how should she do this? The actress playing the part should never move simply because the director tells her. She must find a *motivation* in the character she is playing. Every actor knows that if he is in doubt about a speech or a movement he should not initially ask a question beginning with 'How –?' or 'When –? or 'Where –?', but always 'Why –?'

In this case the question must be – '*Why* does Linda turn away from Biff?' The answer is obvious and is contained within the speech itself. Linda is worried about Willy and angry with Biff. He seems to her to be trying to avoid serious discussion by talking about her appearance. All the painful matters that she is going to tell the boys are already agitating her and she is wondering how she is going to break the news to them. She is anxious for Willy's very life and is beginning to foresee a future in which Willy will be dead and she will have to sell the house. Once the actress has looked ahead to see what Linda is *thinking* and *feeling* at this moment, it becomes much more easy for her to speak the lines as the writer intended.

In the theatre, as in real life, people often feel more than they say. Sometimes they say one thing and think something different. Sometimes, people say nothing, but think a great deal. The words spoken by the characters of any play are usually no more than the surface layer of communication. Below them, the audience can usually see what the characters are really thinking and feeling. Technically, the words actually spoken in a play are called the *text* and the underlying pattern of thoughts and feelings is known as the *undertext*. Go through the extract trying to arrive at a prepared reading, possibly for other people to watch and comment upon. Find the right questions to answer about moves and gestures but remember such answers should always be in terms of the *motivations* of the characters.

Do not forget the characters who have little or nothing to say. In this extract for instance, what is Happy's *undertext* throughout the action?

8 CRITICAL COMMENTS

Of the first production in New York and London, with Lee J. Cobb as Willy Loman in New York and Paul Muni in London, the critics said:

> There is almost nothing to be said for Willy Loman who lies to himself as to others, has no creed or philosophy of life beyond making money by making buddies and cannot even be faithful to his helpful and long suffering wife.
>
> IVOR BROWN

> Willy . . . a good man who represents the homely, decent, kindly virtues of a middle-class society.
>
> BROOKS ATKINSON

> *Death of a Salesman* is a play to make history.
>
> HOWARD BARNES

> . . . the first night congregation made no effort to leave the theatre at the final curtain call. For a period . . . a silence hung over the crowded auditorium. Then, tumultuous appreciation shattered the hushed expectancy.
>
> RICHARD WATTS

> . . . only the most fatuous observer could think of *Death of a Salesman* as a propaganda play.
>
> WILLIAM HAWKINS

> One cannot term the chronology a flashback technique because the transitions are so immediate and logical.
>
> ROBERT COLEMAN

The critics were almost unanimous in finding the play 'moving' and 'significant'. Many critics mention the audiences weeping.

Of the most recent production in New York with Dustin Hoffman as Willy, the critics said:

> As if coming from a pit strewn with stones, the voice retains an actor's strength while expressing a prematurely old man's rage and exhaustion. Looking like any suit would be too large, Mr. Hoffman resembles a clothed skeleton . . . He plays him from the inside out in the American naturalist tradition . . . Willy is the victim of his own evasions as well as false values.
>
> HOLLY HILL

> Hoffman embodies every self-deluded sucker who has sold his soul on the instalment plan. His father made flutes and sold them. Willy makes nothing and sells what?
>
> JACK KROLL

> The character was altered from a 'shrimp' to a 'walrus' to suit Cobb. Hoffman is a sharp-featured shrimp constantly dwarfed by his two sons and having to stretch even to kiss the Woman in the hotel room.
>
> MICHAEL BILLINGTON

> Hoffman looks like an elderly tortoise that has lost its shell. He has an air of inevitable defeat.
>
> CLIVE BARNES

Other comments on the play:

> Miller, though he would obviously like to sympathise with Willy, is essentially and perhaps rightfully contemptuous of him.
>
> HOWARD KISSELL

> I see the play as two entities – an encyclopedia of information about the man (i.e. Willy Loman) and a free-form concentrating my awareness of life up to that point. What it means depends on where on the face of the earth you are and what year it is.
>
> ARTHUR MILLER

(Quoted by Richard Schicksel, *Time Magazine* 1984)

> . . . The critical plot is touched, not lightly, with B-movie melodrama.
>
> DENNIS CUNNINGHAM

> It is not Willy's death that moves us; it's Biff's decision to go on living.
>
> FRANK RICH

. . . *Death of a Salesman* is a masterpiece of concentrated irony and controlled indignation.

LAURENCE KITCHEN

It creates a world and takes us into it. It gives off a feeling of sincerity . . . The little theme is made to take itself too seriously. In this sense it is sentimental.

T. C. WORSLEY

Willy Loman is licked from the start.

LAURENCE KITCHEN

Willy fails to distinguish between popularity and self-respect.

CHRISTOPHER BIGSBY

There has been very little negative criticism of the play whenever or wherever it has been presented. Some critics have pointed out that Miller may be contemptuous of Willy and it is perhaps the acid accuracy of the character drawing that may absolve the play from the charge of sentimentality.

In general, critics have remained impressed by the almost perfect marriage of *form* and *content*.

The film version, with Fredric March (1951), was not an outstanding success and Miller himself did not like it. It is unlikely, however, that any film version could ever be completely successful because the play is so essentially theatrical. It is generally regarded by actors and directors as being a major challenge to their artistic skill. Since it was first produced forty years ago, it is true to say that *Death of a Salesman* began at the top and has remained there ever since.

From the first commercial success in the theatre with *All My Sons* in 1948, until the present day, Miller's reputation with the general public has passed through several phases.

In the 1950s, he was widely known in Europe and America as an innovating playwright and also as a courageous critic of what was seen as an intolerant political establishment in his own country. He was also gladly accepted as an ally by the Royal Court Theatre in London, in 1956, in the battle against the British theatre censor. In the 1960s, his image changed, first with his marriage to Marilyn Monroe and again with his present marriage. Since then his plays have been concerned more with the actions of individual people and less capable of political interpretation than they originally were. Miller has now withdrawn from the eye of the general public although he continues to appear as visiting speaker at many universities.

REVISION QUESTIONS

These questions may be used for examination practice or as topics for revision:

1. How does the playwright make it possible for the audience to see 'inside Willy's head'?

2. How far is it true to say that *Death of a Salesman* is a modern tragedy?

3. How far is the theatrical effect of the play dependent upon the setting, lights and music?

4. Why do you think the playwright chose to use the *timeswitch* as part of his narrative technique?

5. 'Willy fails to distinguish between popularity and self-respect.' Comment on this statement giving examples from the text of the play.

6. How far is it true to say that Biff Loman is the real central character of the play?

7. Comment upon the contributions made by minor characters, such as Bernard, Charley or Howard Wagner, to the chains of causation in the plot.

8. Compare and contrast the two Loman brothers and comment on their relative importance to the storyline.

9. Explain how it is that a play which appears to be so specifically American has achieved such worldwide success.

10. Biff says that Willy 'had the wrong dream'. Comment on this, giving specific examples to support your point of view.

11. Miller believes that a playwright should be 'the poet in the theatre'. How far can *Death of a Salesman* be called a 'poetic play'?

12. How far do you agree that Linda Loman is a very conventionally drawn character?

13. Do you consider the play to be about social morality or a piece of political propaganda? Justify your opinion by reference to the text.

FURTHER READING

Apart from this book, there is no other work devoted exclusively to *Death of a Salesman*. The following all make extensive references to the play.

Bigsby, C. W. E. *A Critical Introduction to Twentieth Century American Drama,* Vol. 2 (Cambridge: Cambridge University Press, 1985).
Carson, N. *Arthur Miller* (London: Macmillan, 1982).
Corrigan, R. W. *Arthur Miller. A Collection of Critical Essays* (Englewood Cliffs, NJ: Prentice-Hall, 1969).
Hogan, R. *Arthur Miller* (Minneapolis: University of Minnesota Press, 1964).

Miller's own account of his experiences while directing the play in China will be found in *Salesman in Beijing* (London: Methuen, 1983).

Drama in Practice (London: Macmillan, 1985), by the present writer, includes a chapter of suggestions for the student actor approaching the play.

All references are to the play in the Penguin edition, first published by Penguin Books in 1949 and reprinted subsequently.

Mastering English Literature

Richard Gill

Mastering English Literature will help readers both to enjoy English Literature and to be successful in 'O' levels, 'A' levels and other public exams. It is an introduction to the study of poetry, novels and drama which helps the reader in four ways – by providing ways of approaching literature, by giving examples and practice exercises, by offering hints on how to write about literature, and by the author's own evident enthusiasm for the subject. With extracts from more than 200 texts, this is an enjoyable account of how to get the maximum satisfaction out of reading, whether it be for formal examinations or simply for pleasure.

Work Out English Literature ('A' level)

S.H. Burton

This book familiarises 'A' level English Literature candidates with every kind of test which they are likely to encounter. Suggested answers are worked out step by step and accompanied by full author's commentary. The book helps students to clarify their aims and establish techniques and standards so that they can make appropriate responses to similar questions when the examination pressures are on. It opens up fresh ways of looking at the full range of set texts, authors and critical judgements and motivates students to know more of these matters.